THE ALASKA FROM SCRATCH COOKBOOK

SEASONAL. SCENIC. HOMEMADE.

WRITTEN & PHOTOGRAPHED BY

MAYA WILSON

RODALE

RODALE
wellness

Live happy. Be healthy. Get inspired.

Sign up today to get exclusive access to our authors, exclusive bonuses, and the most authoritative, useful, and cutting-edge information on health, wellness, fitness, and living your life to the fullest.

Visit us online at RodaleWellness.com
Join us at RodaleWellness.com/Join

Mention of specific companies, organizations, or authorities in this book does not imply endorsement by the author or publisher, nor does mention of specific companies, organizations, or authorities imply that they endorse this book, its author, or the publisher.

Internet addresses and phone numbers given in this book were accurate at the time it went to press.

Rodale books may be purchased for business or promotional use or for special sales. For information, please e-mail: BookMarketing@Rodale.com.

Printed in China

Rodale Inc. makes every effort to use acid-free ∞, recycled paper ♻.

Photographs by Maya Wilson, except those by Danae Wilson on pages 52–53, 110, 155, 200, 201, 217, and all photos of the author

Recipe on front cover: Spicy Chorizo Red Lentil Soup with Kale, page 51

Recipes on back cover: (bottom, right) Hunter's Pie, page 137, and (bottom, left) Salmon Burgers with Sesame Slaw and Wasabi Mayo, page 73

Illustrations by Diane Tusi

Book design by Rae Ann Spitzenberger

Library of Congress Cataloging-in-Publication Data is on file with the publisher.

ISBN 978-1-63565-063-1 hardcover

Distributed to the trade by Macmillan

2   4   6   8   10   9   7   5   3   1   hardcover

Follow us @RodaleBooks on 🐦 📘 📌 📷

We inspire health, healing, happiness, and love in the world.
Starting with you.

DEDICATED TO MY
GRANDMA SUSAN,
WHO MADE THE
KITCHEN MY SAFE
PLACE AND FILLED
IT WITH MUSIC

CONTENTS

FOREWORD

MAYA WILSON'S BELOVED BLOG, *ALASKA FROM SCRATCH*, INTRODUCED me to a woman who had uprooted her life from the sunny shores of California to the wilderness of Southcentral Alaska. In her kitchen on the Kenai Peninsula, she found both a place to call home and a sounding board for a voice that for too long had been silenced.

When I first met Maya, I, too, had recently moved to Anchorage, a place that had never been on my wanderlust radar or bucket list. Of the large and rowdy group of food lovers and chefs, I was most drawn to Maya's calm energy; I understood in that first evening that here was a woman who had lost so much and yet in her new home had found a way to transform grief into something nourishing and joyful.

"Some losses are huge and sudden," Maya writes. "The kind that shock you and take your breath away, happening in a moment and leaving you never the same. . . . It's hard to know who you might have been without the loss because it has seemingly always been there."

If we are lucky, we are able to look through to the other side, to all that there is to gain and the joy to be had from that discovery. Maya came to joy later in life—she, like myself, came to accept that happiness can sometimes be something we choose. And in this case, the old adage is true: Better late than never.

Alaskans can be welcoming yet wary of the outsider; once they let you in, however, they can be at turns warm and quirky, frank and exuberant. To embrace this land is to embrace its harsh beauty—the majestic peaks of the mountain ranges, a back country that is unforgiving but will reward you with a lifelong bounty of indelible moments rich with surprise and beauty.

Not only is this book a love song to the wondrous landscape that is Alaska, but Maya's story and recipes—everything from Smoked Salmon Pot Pie and Chocolate Mint Earthquake Cake to Key Lime Cheesecake with Pretzel Crust and Cashew Horchata—

that she has so generously shared burst with flavor and color.

It took me some time and lots of exceptional five-element acupuncture to finally understand that in order to live this life, in this place, mindfully and joyfully, I needed to no longer lament all that was missing—friends in other parts of the world, readily available ingredients from warmer climes—and finally open my eyes to all that I had gained, including new, deep friendships; the privilege of living in one of the most beautiful landscapes; and a new family.

Maya is one of those important friendships. And this cookbook, like she, is no ordinary adventure. She has taken what's "missing" or "unavailable" in Alaska and, true to the kitchen wizard that she is, created her own food, and a new life. Hers is the story of an arduous emotional journey, a tale of caution to those of us who ignore what's deepest and true inside our hearts.

Because she is like many of us who find solace in the kitchen, in the act of creating a dish to feed and nurture, Maya is right there with us. She's an authoritative guide who offers her own story, unvarnished. Whether guiding us through the healing process of making gnocchi or sharing her sheer delight in baking a cake from scratch, Maya folds us into the warmth of her home like the many layers of a rich and buttery puff pastry.

"In all of the hardest moments of my life," she writes, "cooking has always helped me find my way back home."

Alaska from Scratch could also be called *Life from Scratch*. We live in shaky times, on shaky ground, but cooking is inclusive, a way of gathering disparate cultures and people to a common table. The kitchen is Maya's terra firma where she generously offers up a menu of comfort foods that both ground and transport. So, wherever you may be in the world, as you cook your way through this book, may you find your own sense of home.

–KIM SUNÉE, 2017

"All the magic is in the space between mountains,
where we have to unbecome everything
we thought we were and start from scratch."

–GLENNON DOYLE

INTRODUCTION

"P.S. You should write a cookbook."

JUST LIKE THAT, SHE SAID IT, HANDWRITTEN IN PEN ON CREAMY OFF-white lined paper. She discreetly placed the letter on the kitchen counter just before she left Alaska on a flight back to San Diego. She knew I was sure to find it there waiting in the kitchen after our tear-soaked goodbye in the driveway. At the very bottom of the note, I found this simple postscript, disguised as an afterthought, but very much not. That pesky little *P.S.* carried so much weight for me and stirred me to the core, just precisely as she knew it would.

Everyone needs someone like her in their life—that one person who pushes you, believes in you, fights for you, continually reminds you, "You have it in you." The one who has a way of getting you to verbalize all of the things inside of you that do not yet have words, the person who sees the unwritten book within and demands you let it out. We all need at least one person who helps us find the courage to lean into exactly whom we were meant to be.

Amid the chaos of my three young children on vacation from school, the bustle of summer houseguests, and the frantic clicking of my springer spaniel's paws on the wood floors, I swirl about the kitchen preparing dinner for eight—a large pot of ginger peanut hoisin noodles fit for a crowd. The unmistakable aroma of garlic lingers heavily in the air. I grab my stack of mismatched Alaska pottery bowls and dish up pile after pile of glistening noodles tangling together with cilantro and scallions.

"Who wants chopsticks?" I call out to no one in particular and everyone at once, holding about a dozen of them in my hand. "Don't forget the Sriracha,"

I suggest, nodding my head in the general direction of the essential red bottle as I continue to plate the last of the food. Someone eagerly jumps up and grabs it, transferring it to the table, where it gets passed around.

All the seats are now full, including the dark wood piano bench from downstairs that creates extra space for guests. The overabundant summer sunlight pours in the unshaded windows, casting everything in gold, illuminating the shapes of the tall evergreen trees just outside. A hush falls over the house as I look on from behind the kitchen counter, that sudden quiet when everyone contentedly comes to rest at the table and begins to eat. I live for that moment. I pause to soak it in, slowly scanning the room to make sure everyone has what they need. Then, finally, I let out a deep breath and lean over the counter to rest my legs, taking a couple of bites of noodles.

One head turns and watches me from the dining room. She stops eating midbite and keeps looking in my direction, waiting. Her eyes break away, scanning the table briefly, a flicker. "Maya, come sit with us," she urges. Two other guests look up from their bowls, suddenly aware, and they chime in. One of them jumps up to locate a chair for me. I lower my head, my face flushed with embarrassment, and wave my hand dismissively to say I'm

fine. She insists with her eyes. I reluctantly agree as another chair is placed and I am out of excuses.

This was the day I realized there was no place for me at my own table.

Somewhere along the way I had become like Mrs. Patmore on *Downton Abbey* who pours her life into preparing and serving dinner each day, but never emerges from the downstairs kitchen, where she can be found eating leftovers and washing dishes. I was hiding in plain sight. The food was the representation of me at the table, but I had become invisible. I hadn't set a place for myself, nor had I demanded one be made for me. I was nourishing others but didn't feel worthy of the same nourishment myself.

That night over those noodles, someone saw me. She didn't just see the Maya leaning over the kitchen counter, but she saw the little Maya within, the child with food insecurity standing in the schoolyard trying not to look longingly at everyone else's lunch. The little girl who quietly hoped someone would share their sandwich, yet who felt deeply ashamed when someone actually did.

So I set out in life, rather subconsciously, to fill that empty stomach by nourishing those around me, attempting to ensure that no one I loved would ever know that same sense of hunger, unworthiness, lack of belonging, or shame. I strive to feed people, take care of them, and make them feel safe and at home. When I open up my kitchen, I open up myself, and somehow that vulnerable girl within me feels a little bit fuller and a little less small.

Writing this book is a daily exercise in making a place for myself at the table.

Come sit with me.

FOOD PHILOSOPHY

There are a few things I'd like you to know about me and my food philosophy as you read this book. I live in a modest three-bedroom rental home on the Kenai Peninsula with my family of five, along with our dog, Rosie. My kitchen is not large; my appliances are not new; my countertops are not big, and they are not made of marble. Or granite. Or butcher block. Although I think all of those are splendid and beautiful. I don't have a lot of expensive kitchen equipment or an expansive collection of dishes and props. Heck, I don't even have a pantry. I have a lazy Susan inside of a low cupboard that I use as a makeshift pantry. We bought our dining room table on clearance, and it seats all of us comfortably in the small dining space adjacent to the kitchen. I do nearly all of my cooking, eating, and food styling in these spaces. While it may not be fancy, it is cozy and simple and adequate. There is ample space for both food and memo-

ries to be made. There is plenty of room for love and nourishment to take place. That's all I really need. The rest is gravy.

I like to think that I'm not so different from your average working mother of three. On school days, I'm the earliest riser. The coffeepot is my alarm clock, and I wake up to the smell of dark roast brewing and the faint sounds of trickling and intermittent puffs of steam. I'm up at 5:30 a.m. drinking my first cup of coffee in an attempt to ready myself for the long day ahead. I proceed to wake up the kids one by one, make breakfast, and pack three very standard sack lunches. While it's still dark, I drive my kids to the bus stop in my Subaru Outback with the cracked windshield. A great many windshields in Alaska are cracked. It's a thing. I imagine it's due to the frigid temperatures and all the gravel roads tossing rocks around. One hardly knows, but it adds to my Subaru's rugged Alaska-ness, so I embrace it. Most mornings, my wife and I sit together at the table over the crossword puzzle, coffee in hand. My second cup, her first. Mine with vanilla creamer, hers black. We then enjoy a small breakfast—almost always a couple of eggs on a shared plate, two forks.

If I have a deadline for my newspaper column looming, I'll go straight from the bus stop to the local market, shuffling into the store in my fuzzy slippers and sweatpants, with a knit beanie on my head, to pick up a few ingredients for recipe testing. The grocers all know me there, greet me warmly, and joke about how often I visit the store, but none of them have any idea what I do for a living. No one has ever asked, and it's not usually information I volunteer. I go incognito. Anonymity is hard to come by in this small town, and in Alaska in general, so I tend to guard it fiercely whenever I can find it.

When I pull back into my driveway after shopping, my retired neighbor across the street might be shoveling snow. When he sees me, he'll wave to me, his big yellow dog somewhere nearby. I might offer him some baked goods in exchange for bringing his snow blower over and clearing my driveway. His face will light up and he will gladly oblige. Because in Alaska, we help each other out, trading one kindness for another.

At the end of the day, there is nothing particularly glamorous about this pajama-clad food writing gig of mine. If I can make this food, you can make it, too. I am self-taught. I grew up reading cookbooks and devouring cooking shows, and I have always had an unquenchable curiosity about ingredients, new flavors, and the food preferences of those around me. I collect people's food preferences like a secret recipe box stashed inside my head. I pride myself on knowing both the favorite and most despised flavors of my friends, family, and guests. I am well acquainted with their food allergies and diet restrictions, too. I suppose it's the way I'm wired.

To help best convey my food philosophy, allow me to address some of the questions I am frequently asked by readers.

WHY DO YOU COOK?

I cook to nourish those I love. I have an insatiable need rooted somewhere deep within me for people to be well fed and taken care of. While we can't always know why we become who we become, I imagine that this need I feel is largely the result of the food insecurity I experienced throughout my childhood. I learned to cook at an early age out of necessity—to make something out of nothing, much out of little. In preschool and kindergarten, I would make the kitchen my play space, using canned goods as building blocks, and singing lullabies to the pots and pans before tucking them in underneath kitchen towels and shutting the cupboards at the end of the day.

Goodnight dishes. Goodnight dishes. Goodnight dishes. It's time to go to sleep . . .

One of the first things I ever remember making as a kindergartener in our

Pasadena kitchen is a mayonnaise sandwich—a smear of mayonnaise on white bread. When we were out of bread, a pat of butter (Ahem. Who am I kidding? It was margarine.) on a microwaved flour tortilla was another one of my go-to's. In elementary school, I was a pro at the just-add-water pancake mix, blue boxes of macaroni and cheese, and packages of Top Ramen that cost only pennies at the time.

My mother had a special concoction she called Ogg Nog Mush Mog, which was a box of macaroni and cheese with a little ground beef and canned corn mixed in, a makeshift Hamburger Helper of sorts. Occasionally we would splurge and get the fancier box of macaroni and cheese with the squeezable cheese product in the shiny foil package tucked inside. I remember getting really excited about little things like that. If there was something sweet, my mother liked wiggly brightly colored Jell-O gelatin, sometimes with canned fruit or nuts or cottage cheese mixed in. Her specialty Jell-O mold for Valentine's Day was red gelatin with cinnamon Red Hots candies stirred in, then studded with cubes of cream cheese and walnuts. Or lumpy instant pudding, usually chocolate. Just add milk and stir. My mother loved the thick layer of film that would form on top of

the pudding when it was left uncovered, so she never covered it. These were my survival foods, the flavors of my childhood.

When I was 11 and living in Lincoln City, Oregon, I recall taking all of my mother's food stamps and riding my bicycle to the store, where I bought as much food as I could possibly carry, including jars and jars of baby food for my new little half-brother. On the way home, I dangled the bags from my handlebars. The bike wobbled, bags broke, food fell onto the asphalt, but somehow I managed to get it all back to our single-wide trailer before dark. I made dinner that night, although I don't recall what it was. Probably one of my mother's favorites, like tuna noodle casserole, to try to make her happy, ever the people-pleaser. Those around me were going to be fed, and I was bound and determined to make it happen, even at a young age.

There were many days I went to school without breakfast and with no money for lunch. I would come home from school and plop down in front of the television to watch cooking shows on PBS, before the Food Network was even a thing, learning how to make food I didn't have. I experimented with what was around, often gussying up a store-bought jar of spaghetti sauce, attempting to elevate it to something more than it was. By high school, I would get a ride with a friend to Taco Bell and hope that my then boyfriend had an extra 79 cents to spare so I could get myself a bean burrito, which he often did. When I was invited to friends' houses after school, I could usually be found helping to cook dinner or washing dishes, and I was thankful for the opportunity to just sit at their tables and eat. I would confound my friends by adding a generous swipe of margarine to a bagel before topping it with cream cheese or by adding a big blob of it to my bowl of ramen noodles, just to get more calories. I'm pretty sure they just thought it was weird, but I would insist that it was delicious. I never admitted that it was because I was starving.

Because of my upbringing, I'm not a food snob. While many of the foods I ate throughout my childhood may not have been all that nutritious or even appetizing, they kept me alive, and therefore, I have a deep appreciation for them. To this day, I am not entirely above boxed macaroni and cheese (admittedly I prefer the organic, all-natural option), which ironically is my daughter's current favorite food, despite having a food writer for a mother. Life has quite a sense of humor that way. Even in adulthood, when money has been tight, I've returned to these foods to make it by, although I admit to adding several more ingredients to my ramen noodles now than the packages call for, like vegetables, sesame oil, and Sriracha, sans margarine. And sometimes I still get a nostalgic hankering for Taco Bell, although Taco Bell in Alaska never quite tastes the same as it did back then.

More than anything, I cook because I want people to be fed and satisfied, and to know that inexplicable sense of wholeness that only a homemade meal made with love can provide. As a recipe developer, I get the privilege of feeding more and more people every day vicariously through each person who makes one of my dishes. It's a dream come true for someone like me.

IS YOUR FOOD EXCLUSIVELY FOR ALASKANS?

Absolutely not. I'm not the type of person who thinks that any food should be exclusively for anybody. Food and flavors are meant to be experienced and shared, and our tables and palates are meant to be expanded. As you'll read later in this book, I've lived in several states, and my food reflects some of each of those places. My blog has readers all over the world. One of my fans who has been with me the longest and has, to my knowledge, cooked more of my recipes than anyone else lives in France and keeps in touch often. My weekly food column in the newspaper is similar. I often get emails from readers trying my recipes from all over the country and beyond. These recipes are for you, wherever you are.

WILL I HAVE TROUBLE FINDING INGREDIENTS TO MAKE YOUR RECIPES?

You probably won't need many hard-to-find ingredients. If I can find it in small-town Alaska, then you'll likely be able to find it where you are. The things I can't always locate here on the Kenai Peninsula, like vanilla bean paste for my London Fog recipe, I often order online from somewhere with free shipping to Alaska, like Amazon. If I'm using an unusual item, I'll try to guide you to where you might locate it. If I'm using an Alaska-specific ingredient, like moose or reindeer sausage, I'll be sure to suggest an equally delicious alternative for readers who live elsewhere. The only exception is the wild Alaska seafood featured in this book. It's widely available, and if you can get your hands on it where you live, I highly recommend it. In my mind, there's really nothing that compares to wild-caught seafood straight from Alaska waters.

HOW LONG DO YOUR RECIPES TAKE?

Time-wise, most of my recipes won't require you to be in the kitchen all day. The few exceptions are labors of love and are worth the effort. But, if I need to pick up the kids from the bus stop, drop off prescriptions, and go to a hockey game, I'm sure you probably have other things to do, too. Some of my recipes are quick and easy. But do bear in mind that cooking from scratch does require more time than grabbing takeout or heating up something ready-made. It's absolutely worth it. I'm here to help.

IS YOUR FOOD DIFFICULT TO MAKE?

It's my hope to make cooking from scratch less intimidating and more accessible for families like mine. My food, like my personality, isn't usually fussy. I'm more the down-to-earth type, and I hope that most of my recipes reflect that same approachability. I want my food to be memorable because it's tasty and nourishing and comforting, not because of trendy techniques or impressive plating.

Nothing about life is perfect, and food doesn't need to be perfect either. Food shows up in the messiness of our daily lives, grounding and sustaining us through all the moments, whether mundane or celebratory or grief-stricken. Amid the noise and chaos of the daily grind, we should be able to come to rest at the table. Oftentimes cooking and enjoying a homemade meal can be therapeutic at the end of a hard day. I want people to feel welcome, to kick their feet up, and to have the freedom to be themselves around

my food. If that means you forgo setting the table, blast some music and dance in the kitchen, get food on your face, or eat with your fingers, then by all means do. You've come to the right place. No shame here. So much of life is difficult; the process of making food and feeding those we love doesn't have to be. More than anything, I want it to be a fun, rewarding, and yummy experience.

That being said, there is a great deal of joy and satisfaction to be found when we conquer our kitchen demons: when we triumph over a recipe we once found impossible or intimidating, when we successfully try an ingredient we've avoided for years, or when we have the courage to try a method we think only the professionals can pull off and find we are more capable than we ever thought. We can do hard things. Don't be afraid to try. I've gained so much confidence in the kitchen over the years, and I want to help you do the same. Start where you're comfortable and grow from there. There are recipes in this book for most every skill level, so I'm hopeful you'll find some that suit you, whatever your comfort level in the kitchen. There are hundreds more recipes on my blog to choose from, too.

CAN I MAKE ADAPTATIONS AND SUBSTITUTIONS TO YOUR RECIPES?

I always encourage experimentation, creativity, and ingenuity in the kitchen, as that's how we learn and grow as cooks and gain a better understanding of flavor profiles. It's also how we make the food our own, based on our own sensibilities and preferences. Kitchen experiments, even and maybe especially the failed ones, have taught me a great deal over the years

about what works and what doesn't in the culinary scheme of things. But please understand that I can't guarantee the results when you make changes to a recipe. I likely haven't tried it your way to be able to know for sure if it will work. If I've tried certain substitutions or different methods, I'll usually mention it in the headnote at the top of the recipe. When in doubt, make the recipe as written once before making changes; that way, you have a baseline to which you can compare any future attempts.

ARE YOUR RECIPES HEALTHY? WHAT ABOUT ALLERGIES AND DIETARY RESTRICTIONS?

Everyone defines healthy differently, according to their upbringing, their context, or the dietary needs of those in their household. For some, healthy means eating whole foods or exclusively organic; for others, it means low-carb or low-fat. I offer a wide variety of recipes that cover the spectrum. For example, sometimes my food is very naturally gluten- or dairy-free. Other times my recipes are vegetarian or even vegan, or can be easily adapted to be. I'm not trying to be any of these things in particular. I'm more of an all-around sort of cook.

There was once a time several years back when I received two very different emails from readers in the same week. The first reader stated that my recipes were "too healthy." A few days later, I received an email from someone else declaring that my recipes weren't "healthy enough." I laughed to myself. I learned early on, both as a mother of three picky eaters and as a food writer, that it's impossible to please everyone at the same time. In blogging and food writing, there is always the temptation to lose yourself to the critics, to follow this food trend or that diet fad, or to try to cook exactly like that one celebrity chef or that super-famous blogger, or to buy every shiny new Spiralizer or Instant Pot or sous vide immersion circulator. There are so many voices out there to choose from, specialists in all different cuisines and all different dietary needs and all different techniques. It's been important for me to learn to listen to my readers and stay true to myself at the same time, to remember where I came from, and to cook *my food*—the food that is uniquely and utterly *Alaska from Scratch*. Otherwise, my voice gets lost and my influence diminishes. I have only this one voice. And it's taken me years to learn how to use it and to have the courage to do so, both in food and in life. If my food is too healthy for some and not healthy enough for others, then I'm probably just exactly where I want to be.

Personally speaking, I love my fair share of local fruit and vegetables, wild-caught salmon packed with omega-3s, a big kale salad, and protein-rich quinoa. I also love several cups of dark roast coffee with glugs of sweet creamer on the daily, a plate of pasta in a velvety rich sauce, crusty artisan bread dipped in extra-virgin olive oil and balsamic or slathered with soft butter, and a glass of rosé or a Moscow Mule. I love for my food to be well seasoned and think just about everything needs more salt. And it's a well-known fact that I possess a sweet tooth the size of the State of Alaska and hardly ever end the day without dessert. I love all the delicious things *in moderation.* Especially when they come paired with delicious company and conversation.

My philosophy is that if we are getting into the kitchen and gathering together around the table with wholesome food made from scratch, then we are already eating better, and thereby living healthier lives. That's a huge win in my book. I'm also a big believer in variety at the table. If we are trying new things and if the food we are eating is vibrant—full of different colors and textures and flavors—then not only are we regularly exposing our family and friends to new food experiences, but we are also probably offering up a more diversified, well-balanced diet as a result.

THESE ARE A FEW OF MY FAVORITE THINGS . . .

I'd be remiss if I didn't introduce you to some of my absolute favorite ingredients and kitchen tools.

EGGS

Cue "Single Ladies" by Beyoncé. If you liked it, then you shoulda put an egg on it. While many food fads come and go, hanging on only a couple of years, or maybe even just a couple of months before fizzling out (goodbye, Unicorn Frappuccino), I predict this may come to be known as the Decade of the Egg. What all started with eggs on pizza and eggs on burgers several years ago quickly swelled into innovative egg cooking tutorials galore, baked eggs à la shakshuka, and picture-perfect soft-cooked eggs on ubiquitous avocado toast. And for very good reason. Eggs are power food. One egg contains about 7 grams of high-quality protein, and eggs are packed full of vitamins and nutrients. With the massive rise of cage-free and urban chicken coops, eggs are fresher and more widely and locally available than ever before. I love a flat of fresh eggs—the way they vary in color and size; the way the shells are firmer and more difficult to crack than store-bought; the deep golden color and rich, velvety texture of the yolk; and that undeniable fresh egg flavor that you can know only if you've tried it.

Eggs are one of the most versatile ingredients in a cook's arsenal. There are countless ways to cook and use them, from the sexiest, most luxurious of dishes in the finest of restaurants, to the simplest everyday plate of scrambled eggs and cheese for a hungry toddler. And with a low price point, quick cooking times, and no thawing or prep work required, eggs have saved my bacon time and again when I've needed to get a wholesome, filling homemade meal on the table ASAP and haven't had the time to run to the store for ingredients or to pull meat from the freezer. I think eggs are absolutely appropriate for any meal of the day. I love to start my day with protein, so I almost always turn to eggs first for breakfast, whether runny with a generous drizzle of Sriracha, scrambled with cheese and vegetables, as the centerpiece of a savory breakfast sandwich, or wrapped up in a tortilla (see page 15). While these options are great for lunch, too, we can also go the hard-cooked route with a glorified egg salad sandwich with smoked salmon and avocado, or as the protein atop an abundant, crisp green salad. Or try a lovely springtime frittata or quiche. For dinner, baked eggs like my Quinoa and Egg Enchilada Skillet (see page 11) or a poached egg running over a simple plate of pasta or in a steaming bowl of ramen is sure to leave you feeling satisfied.

ALL THE GREEN THINGS

I love fresh green things. Cilantro is my favorite herb, although it's quite a bit more expensive in Alaska than it was in the Lower 48. I'm always willing to make an exception and splurge for cilantro. If you're one of those people who think it tastes like soap, you may not like my cookbook.

Just kidding.

Sort of.

I buy a bunch of cilantro every week and always keep it on hand. I put it on my curries, stir it into my chili, top my noodle bowls with it, mix it into my salad greens, and sprinkle it copiously onto barbecue chicken pizzas and all of my Mexican food. Except flan. Okay, maybe not all of my Mexican food. But just about. I even like it on my watermelon slices, complete with lime juice and chili salt. If you hate cilantro, I'll be sad, but please feel free to omit it.

You're also likely to find a lot of green onions in this book, a.k.a. scallions. I'm rather attached to those, too. Where lots of people tend to shy away from raw onions, green onions are a great alternative for a milder onion flavor and texture. They are a great, quick way to freshen and boost the flavor of a dish. Same with chives, another fresh green thing, which are smaller and even milder. I love those also. And they're fancy and delicate for when I'm feeling more sophisticated. Wink.

Aside from all of those, I'm also a huge fan of fresh basil. I like it mixed into my meatballs, scattered all over my gnocchi (see page 110), with my Thai food, atop ricotta toast, simmered into my strawberry jam, or stirred into my lemonade (see page 167). Flat-leaf parsley isn't too shabby, either. Fresh herbs in general, like thyme, rosemary, and dill, are often the unsung heroes of a dish. Stock up on all the fresh green things. You won't regret it.

AVOCADO OIL

Avocado oil is one of the healthier fats and has an extremely high smoking point, much higher than extra-virgin olive oil. This makes it ideal for getting a beautiful sear on your food, from scallops and salmon, to steak and burgers and chicken, and for caramelizing those vegetables. Don't be afraid of using high heat to get some color on your food. That's where the flavor is. Avocado oil is also neutrally flavored, so you can use it for just about anything without altering the taste.

SALTED BUTTER

I'm an unapologetic and rebellious rule breaker with this one. Where many a chef and baker will tell you to always use unsalted butter so that you can control the salt content of your food, I am a salted butter girl all the way. It's pretty much the only kind I buy. I have never found a dish to be too salty because of

the butter. And I think a little salt in desserts and baked goods is a very good thing. So, in recipes that call for "butter," I'm using salted butter. But feel free to use your preference. If I feel salted butter is essential to the recipe, I'm sure to specify this in the ingredients list.

SRIRACHA

I'm obsessed. I think Sriracha is one of the best ingredients ever, and I always have a bottle on hand. Several years ago when there was a "Sriracha shortage" looming, I stocked up on all the bottles I could find in my corner of Alaska. I love this stuff on eggs, Asian food, seafood, mixed into guacamole, in my mayo, and stirred into my barbecue sauce. My wife even likes it in her ketchup, which she affectionately calls Srirachup. Get thyself a bottle. Or five. You'll want to have it on hand when making several of the recipes in this book.

KITCHENAID STAND MIXER (PREFERABLY WITH TWO MIXING BOWLS)

You will notice that in many of my recipes, I recommend the use of a stand mixer. I didn't get my first basic stand mixer until I had been a mom for almost 10 years, and gosh, I really wish I had gotten one much sooner. It's one of those things in life that I didn't understand the need for, but once I had one, I couldn't imagine my life without it. It revolutionized my cooking and very directly contributed to my gaining confidence in the kitchen. Stand mixers are workhorses and multitaskers. They will not only make working in the kitchen faster and easier, they will also produce a consistent result whether you're making mashed potatoes, whipping up fluffy frosting or a mean meringue, shredding chicken, or kneading bread dough. I strongly recommend getting an additional mixing bowl. Some recipes, like my Chocolate Mint Earthquake Cake (see page 193), call for more than one step in a stand mixer, and it's helpful not to have to stop what you're doing to wash out the mixing bowl for another use.

FISH TWEEZERS

If you're going to be spending some time with the wild Alaska seafood chapter of this book, which I desperately hope you are, I recommend a sturdy pair of fish tweezers. I got myself a pair on Amazon. You'll want them especially for salmon. When in a pinch (pun totally intended), a small regular pair of tweezers will also work.

OFFSET SPATULAS

Offset spatulas are very cool, fun little tools. They are relatively inexpensive, come in different sizes, and make me feel like a professional pastry chef whenever I use them, which I most certainly am not. Arm me with an offset spatula and some frosting, meringue, or melted chocolate, and I can swoop and spread and make pretty little peaks and valleys like the best of them. And I bet you can, too.

MICROPLANE

I'm extremely fond of my microplanes, both at home and when I work in a restaurant kitchen. These suckers are sharp and expedient, bringing loads of flavor to dishes by way of their tiny little shavings. Citrus zest, fresh ginger, whole nutmeg, and Parmesan cheese are just a few of the ways I love to use my microplanes. Just take caution not to get your skin too close. Fair warning.

CHEF'S KNIFE

A solid, well-sharpened chef's knife is an indispensable investment. When you have a good knife upon which to rely, and you've spent a good deal of time using it, you become attached to it. You're much less likely to cut yourself if you're working with a knife with which you're well acquainted. You're also much less likely to cut yourself if you keep your knives sharp, which is counterintuitive, but it's true. A good knife makes you more confident and more efficient when prepping, chopping, slicing, and dicing, all vital parts

of being in the kitchen. Where once I found knife work tedious, I now enjoy it and even find it therapeutic at times, all because I love my knife. Nothing quite builds momentum and energy in the kitchen for me like the rhythm of steel rocking swiftly against a cutting board. That's the moment when I really start to get in the zone.

If there's one thing I learned while working in a restaurant, it's that chef's knives are very personal things and that a chef cares for and protects her knife like it's an extension of herself. All the other cooks in the kitchen know whose knife is whose, based on the brand, the size, or the look of it. You don't ever use another cook's knife without asking. At the end of the day, you tuck your knife in its case and take it home with you, only to bring it back again the next day. You select a knife based on the weight of it and how it feels in your hand, and you want to find one that fits you just right. You keep it clean, you sharpen it regularly, and you are fiercely possessive over it. I'm the type of person to gladly share my knife with the cook beside me when they're in need, but not all cooks are like that. When cooking at home, I have several knives to choose from, but I have a strong favorite and will typically wash my favorite knife for another use before reaching for a different one.

CAST IRON

I'm not sure I'd know what to do without my 12-inch cast-iron skillet and my enameled cast-iron Dutch oven. You'll see cast iron a lot in this book, not only because it's one of the most useful and versatile materials in the kitchen, but also because cast iron is very Alaska, dating back to gold miners and homesteaders. Many home cooks are intimidated by cast iron, and I was once one of them, assuming it was too heavy and high-maintenance for everyday cooking. Boy, was I wrong. Spreading a thin smear of oil into your cast-iron pan after cleaning takes only 10 seconds and will protect your pan from rust. When I worked in the restaurant, we had dozens of tiny cast-iron skillets, and we oiled them every night at the end of service, so I became very proficient at it. If you get an enameled cast-iron pan, there's no extra oiling step required. When you see the gorgeous sear you can achieve on your meat, the golden crispy crust you can get on your pan pizza (page 135), or the way you can transfer the pan from stovetop to campfire to oven without missing a beat, you'll be a cast-iron user for life. If you're new to cast iron, start with a 12-inch skillet. Lodge makes a sturdy, affordable one like the one I use throughout this book.

IPHONE

I hardly ever enter the kitchen without my iPhone. I use it to look up recipes (even my own) and research methods and techniques while cooking. I use it to text friends and family and stay connected as I work. I also use it to listen to music. Finally, I use it to take quick photos of my food and sometimes post them to Instagram.

I have one final note about my food philosophy before we dig in:

CLEAN AS YOU GO

I can't stress this one enough. It's a huge part of who I am as a cook and

the way I move about the kitchen. Cleaning and cooking are not mutually exclusive; they go hand in hand. This isn't just to keep things clean and sanitary (although that's important, don't get me wrong); it's also about reducing the clutter in my mind and in my space and bringing clarity to the process of cooking. My kitchen is a small space, and I want to make it work well for me, not against me. Give yourself room to work and room to breathe. If I step into the kitchen to make a meal, I make sure the sink is empty and the counters are clean before I begin (there's nothing more frustrating than when you need the vegetable peeler in the middle of a recipe and you search endlessly for it only to find it dirty at the bottom of the sink underneath a pile of dishes). When I'm done using an ingredient, I put it away before reaching for the next. When things need to be discarded, I throw them away or recycle them as I go. While the fish is searing, I'm wiping the oil splatter with a kitchen rag, washing the cutting board, and putting dishes in the dishwasher.

This clean-as-you-go thing is just an extension of who I am. I can't really help it. I almost do it without realizing it, intrinsically. This is where things get funny and those who love me like to laugh at me about it. At home, I often hear, "Where did my water glass go?" The answer is always that I mistakenly put it in the dishwasher before my wife was done with it. My kids often protest, "Hey, I wasn't done," when I swoop in to take their ice cream bowls to the sink before they've licked them clean. Once, I made a recipe with rice vinegar, and when I was done, the cap to the bottle was nowhere to be found. I had most likely thrown it away in my efforts to clean up.

When I worked at the restaurant, I would often clean up after my colleagues, too. This was usually appreciated and helpful, but sometimes I would put ingredients or utensils away before they were done with them. "What happened to the chinois? It was just right here." Inevitably, I'd tossed it into the dish pit—in which case, I'd have to wash it and sanitize it as quickly as possible and give it right back. "Where's the mignonette? I wasn't done with it." Of course, I had put it back in the walk-in fridge and would have to go fish it out again. Occasionally this clean-as-you-go method backfires on me. But I have to laugh because it's who I am, pros and cons and all.

1 / ALASKA MORNINGS
BREAKFAST

BREAKFAST

*A*lthough I didn't grow up in Alaska, I have lived here longer than I have ever lived anywhere else in my lifetime. I had 19 different homes before graduating from high school—from my birth in Hawaii, to California, to Oregon, and back to California again. In California alone, I've lived all over the state, from Pasadena to north of Sacramento and back down to San Diego and just about everywhere in between. I chalk this up mostly to a complex cocktail of wanderlust and eccentricity on the part of my late mother, a self-identified hippy, who followed nobody's rules except her own. In those years, she was as unpredictable as she was captivating, and I often received little notice of an impending move to a new location.

When asked where I'm from, I always let out a long sigh and wait to see if people want the real answer, the looooonnnnnng answer. Am I Hawaiian? A California girl? An Alaskan? One hardly knows. If you add in my formative post-college stint in the mountains of Arizona where two of my three children were born, perhaps it's just safer to call me a West Coaster and leave it at that. I have never fit into a neat little regional box, or any boxes at all, really. I'm from everywhere and nowhere. I have hardly ever known where to call home.

One thing I learned from all of this moving from place to place is the exquisite power that food has to make anywhere feel familiar, to make any moment feel like coming home. Breakfast does this for me more than any other meal—the way a bowl steaming with hot cereal or a soft-cooked egg on wheat toast can send me straight back to my early days in Grandma's kitchen, how a lofty stack of tangy buttermilk pancakes dripping with butter and pure maple syrup reminds me of the Saturday mornings I spent with energetic, mess-making toddlers under foot, or how the smell of a fresh pot of coffee brewing while I'm still in bed in the morning can make anywhere smell like exactly where I want to be.

ALASKA MORNINGS ARE THE BEST MORNINGS. THE AIR IS ALWAYS CRISP, SCENTED WITH THE DAY'S NEWNESS, THE CHANGING SEASONS, AND ALASKA'S UNRELENTING LANDSCAPE.

Alaska mornings are the best mornings. The air is always crisp, scented with the day's newness, the changing seasons, and Alaska's unrelenting landscape. Summer has a verdant smell, like lush green mixed with wildflowers and berries. In the coastal towns, like my home on the Kenai Peninsula, the scent of the salty seawater is most prominent in summer, wafting in with the breeze. Some Alaskans swear that they can tell when the salmon are running in July by the smell in the air.

As we shift into fall, the mist rises off of the lakes and streams, dampening the cooler air. I smell yellow leaves, mushrooms and moss, smoke from nearby wood stoves, and petrichor from the autumn rain. The earth is fragrant and forgiving underfoot like used coffee grounds.

The long winter sweeps in with its dark, starry mornings, the air so frosty that your breath catches in your chest when you inhale. In the late morning, the sun rises and lingers low on the horizon, casting a pomegranate red glow across the sky. When the light hits the pure white expanse, the snow sparkles and gleams like sanding sugar, a phenomenon nearly impossible to capture in photographs, but that never seems to stop me from trying.

Alaska mornings lend themselves well to substantial breakfast fare with steaming beverages in large mugs, all best enjoyed in *cozies,* otherwise known as pajamas. Slippers or thick hand-knit wool socks recommended.

STRAWBERRY SHORTCAKE SCONES

Makes 12

I developed this recipe one Alaska spring day when I had some ripe strawberries that needed to be used. They have since become one of my favorite recipes of all time. Years later, when I made my wife's first-ever breakfast in bed, I served these up with a mug of hot black coffee. She now requests them often.

Buttery and golden, these scones are studded with juicy strawberry quarters, then drenched in vanilla cream glaze while still warm from the oven. The trick to a perfect, tender scone is to be content with imperfection—that is to say, don't overwork the dough. Allow it to be a crumbly mess that just barely comes together. The perfection comes later when you take that first bite.

FOR THE STRAWBERRY SCONES:

2 cups all-purpose flour

1 tablespoon baking powder

3 tablespoons sugar

½ teaspoon salt

5 tablespoons chilled butter, cut into ¼" cubes

12 strawberries, hulled and quartered

¾ cup half-and-half

FOR THE GLAZE:

1½ cups confectioners' sugar

2–3 tablespoons half-and-half

½ teaspoon vanilla extract

1 Preheat the oven to 425°F. Line a baking sheet with parchment paper.

2 *To make the strawberry scones:* In a mixing bowl, combine the flour, baking powder, sugar, and salt. Add the butter and cut it in with a pastry blender until the mixture resembles crumbs.

3 Toss in the strawberries and coat them lightly with the flour mixture. Add the half-and-half and fold gently until the mixture just begins to come together and forms a soft, yet shaggy dough. Add more half-and-half if needed to get the dough to come together. Do not knead or overmix the dough, as this will cause the scones to become dense and will smash the strawberries in the process.

4 Turn the dough out onto a floured surface and pat into a 1"-thick rectangle. With a sharp knife, cut the rectangle into 6 squares, then cut the squares on the diagonal to form 12 triangles. Place the scones on the baking sheet and bake for 14 to 16 minutes, or until they are cooked through and golden.

5 Place a sheet of parchment paper on a work surface, then place a cooling rack on top of the parchment. Remove the scones from the pan to the cooling rack. Cool for 10 minutes.

6 *To make the glaze:* Meanwhile, in a medium bowl, whisk together the confectioners' sugar, half-and-half, and vanilla until smooth and slightly runny.

7 Taking each scone by the bottom, dip them top side down directly into the glaze until the top is covered. Return the scones to the cooling rack and allow the glaze to drip down the sides and off the rack onto the parchment. The glaze will firm up as the scones cool. These scones are best enjoyed the same day and are delicious warm.

GINGER BAKED OATMEAL
WITH BLUEBERRIES AND PEARS

Makes 4 to 6 servings

As a child, I didn't realize how lucky I was that Grandma Susan always kept a full collection of hot cereal options in her pantry, from Cream of Wheat to Malt-O-Meal, and from grits to old-fashioned rolled oats. I might have even protested and asked why I couldn't eat cold, colorful, sugary cereals like other kids. How fortunate I was to have someone make me a hot, wholesome breakfast, studded with plump raisins and nuts. Later on, when I no longer lived with Grandma, I missed the hot breakfasts and the care and safety that came with them. As an adult, I often crave a steaming bowl of hot cereal, particularly when I am not feeling well and am in dire need of a dose of comfort and a hug from Grandma.

When it comes to oats, slow and steady wins the race. I opt for the longer-cooking rolled oats over quick oats every time, as quick oats are almost always gluey in texture. But if you're not interested in standing over the stove boiling and stirring your oats in the morning, baking them like this is a great option, particularly if you're cooking for a crowd.

1 large Bartlett pear, quartered and cored

1 cup blueberries

1½ cups rolled oats

¾ teaspoon ground cinnamon

¾ teaspoon ground ginger

¼ teaspoon salt

½ teaspoon baking powder

1½ cups milk

2 eggs

4 tablespoons butter, melted

⅓ cup pure maple syrup

1 teaspoon vanilla extract

FOR SERVING:
Milk

Brown sugar

1 Preheat the oven to 375°F. Grease a 13" x 9" baking dish.

2 Chop three-quarters of the pear into bite-size pieces. Sprinkle the chopped pears evenly in the bottom of the baking dish. Slice the remaining quarter of the pear into thin slices and set them aside to top the oatmeal. Sprinkle ½ cup of the blueberries into the pan with the pears, reserving the rest of the blueberries to put on top.

recipe continues

3 In a mixing bowl, stir together the oats, cinnamon, ginger, salt, and baking powder until combined. Scatter the oat mixture evenly over the fruit in the pan.

4 In another bowl, whisk together the milk, eggs, butter, maple syrup, and vanilla until smooth. Pour the milk mixture evenly over the oats. Top with the pear slices and remaining ½ cup blueberries.

5 Bake for 30 to 35 minutes, or until golden and set. Spoon generous heaps of the baked oatmeal into serving bowls. Pour milk over top of the oatmeal and serve with brown sugar on the side to sweeten, if needed.

QUINOA AND EGG ENCHILADA SKILLET

Makes 4 to 6 servings

My longtime best friend, Kari, loves this recipe from my blog and insisted that it needed to make an appearance in the cookbook. And if you knew Kari like I know her, you'd know that hers is the kind of advice you should always heed. Or else. She's a tough cookie, but an extremely wise one, too.

Consider this my Latin twist on the popular shakshuka, the Moroccan dish of eggs baked into a tomato- and chile-based sauce scented with smoky cumin. My version draws upon my San Diego sensibilities, incorporating quinoa, black beans, and corn baked under a layer of enchilada sauce, melty cheese, and runny eggs. This protein-rich, flavorful, meatless breakfast is outstanding for any meal of the day. Homemade red enchilada sauce is recommended for best flavor (page 143), but when you're in a pinch, a store-bought can of sauce works well.

2 cups cooked quinoa

1 can (15 ounces) black beans, rinsed and drained

1 cup corn

2 tablespoons fresh lime juice (from 1 lime)

2 teaspoons extra-virgin olive oil

1 teaspoon ground cumin

½ teaspoon garlic powder

Salt and ground black pepper

2 cups red enchilada sauce (page 144)

⅔ cup grated Colby Jack cheese

6 eggs

FOR SERVING:

Cilantro, chopped

Green onions, sliced

Avocado pitted, peeled, and sliced

Hot sauce (such as Tapatio) or salsa

1 Preheat the oven to 375°F.

2 In a mixing bowl, combine the quinoa, black beans, and corn. In a small bowl, mix together the lime juice, oil, cumin, and garlic powder. Pour the lime mixture over the quinoa and toss to combine. Season with salt and pepper to taste. Spread the quinoa mixture into the bottom of a 12" cast-iron skillet. Pour the enchilada sauce over the quinoa and sprinkle with the cheese.

3 Make 6 small indentations in the top of the cheese, evenly spacing them out. Crack an egg into each indentation. Season the eggs with salt and pepper to taste. Bake for 20 to 30 minutes, or until the egg whites are completely set but the yolks are still runny, and the edges of the skillet are bubbly.

4 Serve promptly with fresh cilantro, green onions, and avocado slices on top, and hot sauce or salsa on the side.

BREAKFAST TACOS WITH BACON AND KALE

Makes 8

Breakfast tacos are one of my everyday staples; we enjoy them a couple of mornings a week. There's just something that makes me deeply happy about wrapping eggs in a toasty tortilla and topping them with hot sauce. It's a great way to start the day. But I actually first developed this recipe when I was desperate for a quick dinner idea. I had some kale on hand that needed to be used and a few slices of bacon. When you toss the kale briefly in the same pan as the bacon, it turns a deep, shiny green and becomes tender and full of flavor. If you're not a bacon fan, Mexican chorizo would also work well. For the corn tortillas, I place them directly onto the burner of my gas range to char them on both sides. If you don't have that option, I recommend steaming them so that they are warm and pliable.

6 eggs

2 tablespoons milk

Salt and ground black pepper

1 teaspoon butter

3 slices bacon

1 cup finely chopped kale

¼ teaspoon garlic powder

8 yellow corn tortillas, charred on both sides

Hot sauce, such as Tapatío

FOR SERVING (OPTIONAL):

Cheddar cheese, grated

Sour cream

Avocado, pitted, peeled, and sliced

1 In a bowl, whisk together the eggs, milk, and salt and pepper to taste. In a skillet, melt the butter over medium heat. Pour the egg mixture into the pan and stir until set. Transfer the scrambled eggs to a covered dish to keep warm.

2 Wipe out the pan and return it to the heat. Cook the bacon until browned and crisp. Remove the bacon to some paper towels to drain.

3 Pour off all but 2 teaspoons of the bacon fat left over in the pan. Return the pan to the heat and toss in the kale. Season with the garlic powder and salt and pepper to taste. Cook, stirring frequently, for 3 minutes, or until the kale is tender and vibrant green. Crumble the bacon and add it to the kale. Stir in the scrambled eggs. Remove the pan from the heat. Lay out the tortillas on serving plates and spoon the scrambled egg mixture into each of the tortillas. Top with hot sauce. Serve with cheese, sour cream, and avocado slices, if desired.

BREAKFAST SANDWICHES WITH MAPLE MUSTARD SAUCE

Makes 2

I began making maple mustard sauce years ago as a dipping sauce for sweet potato fries and featured it on my blog in my first month of blogging. I found the maple and mustard combination so addicting that I started using this sauce on all sorts of other things, from grilled chicken breasts to hard-cooked eggs to ham sandwiches.

When I cooked at The Flats Bistro in Kenai, Alaska, years later, I was sure to start making my maple mustard sauce for customers. However, in the back of the house, the staff and I frequently made something with it that wasn't on the menu—breakfast sandwiches. We often had leftover English muffins or buttermilk biscuits on hand after Sunday brunch, along with some Canadian bacon from making Eggs Benedict. A Cheddar and Canadian bacon breakfast sandwich with a runny egg slathered with maple mustard sauce became a staff favorite to get us through a busy morning of prep heading into lunch service. I still make them at home.

FOR THE MAPLE MUSTARD SAUCE:

1 tablespoon Dijon mustard

1 tablespoon mayonnaise

1 tablespoon pure maple syrup

FOR THE SANDWICHES:

1 teaspoon butter

2 eggs

Salt and freshly cracked black pepper

¼ cup grated sharp Cheddar cheese

4 slices Canadian bacon

2 English muffins, toasted

¼ cup sliced green onions

1 *To make the maple mustard sauce:* In a small bowl, combine the mustard, mayonnaise, and maple syrup. Whisk until smooth and set aside.

2 *To make the sandwiches:* In a non-stick skillet, melt the butter over medium heat. Crack the eggs into the skillet. Season them with salt and pepper to taste. Top each egg with half of the cheese. Cover and cook, sunny side up, until the cheese is melted, the white is cooked through, and the yolk is still runny. Transfer the eggs to a plate and set aside.

3 Increase the heat to medium high and cook the Canadian bacon for 1 to 1½ minutes, or until brown on the bottom. Turn and cook until brown on the other side.

4 To assemble the sandwiches, place each egg onto half of an English muffin. Top each egg with 2 slices of Canadian bacon. Spoon the maple mustard sauce over the Canadian bacon. Sprinkle with the green onions and gently top the sandwich with the other half of the English muffin, being careful not to break the yolk. Serve promptly with napkins.

SWEDISH PANCAKES WITH LEMON

Makes 9

After living for about 14 months in a small Swedish village in the Central Valley of California shortly after college, I fell in love with the tender, eggy Swedish pancakes featured on just about every breakfast menu. It took me years and many attempts to develop a recipe that replicated them. They became a family favorite, often requested by my oldest son, Brady.

Later, as a brunch chef here in Alaska, I was sure to put my Swedish Pancakes on the menu. I like to serve these with lots of confectioners' sugar and bright, freshly squeezed lemon. However, if you can get your hands on some traditional lingonberry jam, serve that alongside as well with a dollop of sour cream.

5 eggs

1¼ cups milk

3 tablespoons sour cream

1¼ cups all-purpose flour

2 tablespoons sugar

½ teaspoon salt

2 teaspoons neutral-flavored oil, such as vegetable oil + additional as needed

1 lemon, quartered

4 tablespoons butter, melted

Confectioners' sugar

1 In a blender, combine the eggs, milk, and sour cream. Blend until smooth. Add the flour, sugar, and salt and blend until completely smooth. The batter will be thin and pourable.

2 In a medium skillet, heat the oil over medium heat. When the pan and oil are hot, pour ¼ to ⅓ cup of the batter onto the center of the pan. Quickly but gently lift and swirl the pan to spread the batter to the edges. Cook for 60 to 90 seconds, or until the bottom is set. Turn and cook for 30 to 60 seconds, or until the other side sets up and golden

flecks can be seen. Using a spatula, fold the pancake in half and in half again to make a triangle. Set the pancake aside and repeat with the remaining batter, oiling the pan again between pancakes as needed.

3 When ready to serve, lay 3 pancakes on each plate. Drizzle generously with fresh lemon juice and melted butter, then dust liberally with confectioners' sugar. Serve promptly with more lemon wedges, melted butter, and confectioners' sugar on the side.

TWO-POTATO HASH
WITH REINDEER SAUSAGE

Makes 4 to 6 servings

Alaskans love their potatoes, which we grow locally and plentifully. During my days as the Sunday brunch chef at the bistro, potato hash was one of the most popular items. I'd get to the restaurant at 4:00 or 5:00 a.m., and the first thing I'd do is heave bins of chopped potatoes into giant stockpots to parboil. When they were ready, I'd use every ounce of might I had in my small frame to lift the heavy pots full of boiling water and potatoes over to the sink to drain and cool before I'd lay the potatoes out on sheet pans, where I'd season them just so. Later, they'd be fried up to order with peppers and onions until crisp. Although the amazing team of line cooks prepped pound after pound of potatoes for brunch each week, we could hardly ever make enough of it. We often ran out before the end of service, and I could be heard shouting, "Eighty-six hash!" from behind the line. It was just that popular.

Making hash at home is much less labor intensive, but just as delicious. I like to use at least 2 different potato varieties for flavor, color, and texture. My favorites for hash are russets, with the skin still on, and sweet potatoes, peeled. I like to par-bake my potatoes briefly in the oven or microwave. Then I use a hot, well-oiled cast-iron skillet to brown my potatoes until crisp.

One of the most important things to remember when making hash is to always season your potatoes generously. I love lots of salt, cracked black pepper, and Old Bay seasoning. And I like to add my protein, like slices of spicy reindeer sausage, directly to my hash, which gives the potatoes an added layer of flavor. Feel free to use any kind of breakfast protein you prefer, such as pork sausage, bacon, diced ham, or even chorizo. Top your hash with a couple of eggs any style, and you have a substantial, well-rounded meal. Ketchup or hot sauce highly encouraged on the side.

recipe continues

3 russet potatoes, unpeeled

1 medium sweet potato, peeled

2 tablespoons vegetable oil

13 ounces smoked reindeer sausage, sliced

1 red bell pepper, cut into 1" pieces

1 red onion, cut into 1" pieces

2 teaspoons Old Bay seasoning

Salt and cracked black pepper

FOR SERVING:

Green onions, sliced

Hot sauce or ketchup

1 Pierce the potatoes and sweet potato with a fork and microwave on high power for 5 minutes, or until par-baked. You want them to be just tender, but not completely cooked through and soft. When the potatoes are cool enough to handle, chop them into hearty bite-size chunks. Peel the sweet potato and chop it into chunks the same size as the russets. Set the potatoes and sweet potato aside.

2 In a large cast-iron skillet, heat the oil over medium-high heat. Cook the sausage until browned on both sides. Transfer the sausage to a plate and set aside. Add the bell pepper and onion to the pan and cook, stirring often, until the vegetables are tender and begin to brown. Transfer the vegetables to the plate with the sausage and set aside.

3 Add more oil to the pan if needed. Add the potatoes and sweet potato and season them generously with the Old Bay and salt and black pepper to taste. Cook, without stirring, until they develop a crisp brown crust on the bottom. Stir and continue to cook until the potatoes are crisp on at least 2 sides.

4 Return the sausage, bell pepper, and onion to the pan and stir to combine with the potatoes. Taste for seasoning and add more salt and black pepper if needed. Sprinkle with green onions and serve promptly, with hot sauce and/or ketchup on the side.

ORANGE-SCENTED FRENCH TOAST STUFFED WITH NUTELLA

Makes 4 servings

After years of making several versions of French toast both at home and for brunch in the restaurant kitchen, I have learned a few tricks: Rather than using presliced bread, which is thinner and less sturdy, I prefer to cut my own thick slices off of a loaf of French or Italian bread. To achieve beautiful caramelization and browning on the surface of the toast, I like my skillet to be good and hot, around medium-high heat, and swirling with bubbling, melted butter. I almost never leave out the orange zest in the egg batter. The welcome brightness and acidity of the citrus cuts straight through the richness of the dish. I have learned that double-decker stacks of French toast with a surprise filling in the center—whether it be fresh fruit, sweetened cream cheese, or chocolate hazelnut spread—are always the most popular, not to mention playful and impressive. And finally, I love to spike my confectioners' sugar with cinnamon before dusting the toast, a trademark move I learned while managing a small café at a fishing resort high up in California's Eastern Sierra mountains back in 2001. This restaurant-quality breakfast is simple enough to make at home and is sure to make your family and friends feel extravagantly spoiled.

5 eggs

½ cup whole milk

¼ cup freshly squeezed orange juice

2 teaspoons sugar

1 teaspoon vanilla extract

1 teaspoon orange zest

2 tablespoons butter

8 slices French bread

¼ cup Nutella

½ cup confectioners' sugar

1 teaspoon ground cinnamon

FOR SERVING:

Butter

Pure maple syrup

1 Preheat the oven to 150°F.

2 In a shallow dish, whisk together the eggs, milk, orange juice, sugar, vanilla, and orange zest until smooth and well combined.

3 Heat a large skillet over medium-high heat. Swirl 1 tablespoon of the butter in the pan to melt and coat the surface.

recipe continues

4 Briefly dip 1 slice of bread into the egg mixture, then turn it over and dip the other side as well. Promptly transfer the soaked bread directly to the skillet. Repeat with 3 more slices of bread, or until the pan is full but not over-crowded. Cook for 2 minutes, or until the bottoms are browned, caramelized, and crisp. Turn and cook for 2 minutes, or until set in the center. Transfer the French toast to a baking sheet, placing the slices in a single layer. Place the baking sheet in the oven to keep the French toast warm while you cook the remaining slices of bread. Add the remaining 1 tablespoon butter to the hot skillet and repeat the above steps with the remainder of the bread.

5 To assemble the French toast, place 1 slice on a plate. Using a butter knife, spread the slice generously with 1 tablespoon of Nutella. Place another slice of French toast on top. In a small bowl, mix together the confectioners' sugar and cinnamon. Dust the Nutella-stuffed French toast with the cinnamon confectioners' sugar. Repeat with the remaining slices. Serve with butter and pure maple syrup.

TOASTED COCONUT GRANOLA WITH CASHEWS AND CACAO

Makes 4 cups

Homemade granola makes great wilderness food. It's hardy and packable for a day hike on the trail or a weekend camping trip. It's delicious over Greek yogurt, maybe with some fresh fruit, or with milk as breakfast cereal, or just eaten by the handful as a wholesome snack. This version has cashews and raw quinoa, adding both protein and texture. Then I added cacao nibs covered in dark chocolate for a natural little burst of caffeine. My aunt Wendy ships them up to Alaska for me from Trader Joe's. If you can't find the cacao nibs or are hoping to cut back on some of the caffeine, dark chocolate mini morsels would be a nice alternative.

2 cups rolled oats

¼ cup raw quinoa, rinsed and drained

¾ cup cashews, roughly chopped

¾ cup shredded coconut

2 tablespoons firmly packed brown sugar

½ teaspoon ground ginger

⅛ teaspoon ground cinnamon

½ teaspoon salt

½ cup pure maple syrup

¼ cup coconut oil, melted

½ teaspoon coconut extract

¼ cup crystallized ginger, finely chopped

⅓ cup dark chocolate–covered cacao nibs

1 Preheat the oven to 300°F. Line a large rimmed baking sheet with parchment paper.

2 In a mixing bowl, stir together the oats, quinoa, cashews, coconut, brown sugar, ground ginger, cinnamon, and salt until well combined. In a small bowl, combine the maple syrup, coconut oil, and coconut extract. Pour the wet ingredients over the oat mixture and toss to coat well.

3 Spread the mixture evenly onto the baking sheet. Bake for 30 to 40 minutes, stirring every 10 minutes, or until the granola is golden brown, fragrant, and beginning to crisp. The granola will crisp up further as it cools. Cool completely on the pan. Sprinkle the crystallized ginger and cacao nibs evenly over the granola. Store in airtight containers.

BLUEBERRY ZUCCHINI MUFFINS

Makes 18

Two things that Alaska grows well in the summer are zucchini and wild
blueberries. Zucchini grow to enormous, record-breaking sizes due to the
seemingly endless summer sunlight, and blueberries can be found ripe
for the picking all across the state. I've brought the two together in these sweet,
irresistibly moist muffins. With 2 cups each of shredded zucchini and fresh
blueberries, these treats are absolutely bursting with both, boasting
vibrant purple and bright green when you bite in. Even my children who
swear they hate zucchini love these muffins and gobble them up.

3 eggs

1 cup vegetable oil

1 tablespoon vanilla extract

2 cups sugar

2 cups shredded zucchini

2 teaspoons lemon zest

3 cups all-purpose flour

1 teaspoon salt

1 teaspoon baking powder

¼ teaspoon baking soda

1 teaspoon ground cinnamon

2 cups fresh blueberries

*FOR THE CRUMBLE
TOPPING:*

⅓ cup all-purpose flour

⅓ cup sugar

Dash of salt

¼ cup butter, cubed

1   Preheat the oven to 350°F. Grease
two 12-cup muffin pans. Place 18 paper
liners in the pans, if desired.

2   In a mixing bowl, beat together the
eggs, oil, and vanilla. Add the sugar,
zucchini, and lemon zest, stirring
well to combine. In another bowl, stir
together the flour, salt, baking powder,
baking soda, and cinnamon. Add the
dry ingredients to the zucchini mixture and mix together to combine.
Gently fold in the blueberries. Using a

¼-cup measuring cup, scoop the batter
into the muffin pans.

3   *To make the crumble topping:* In a
small bowl, combine the flour, sugar,
and salt. Using a pastry blender, cut in
the butter until the mixture is crumbly.
Sprinkle the crumble topping evenly
over each of the muffins. Bake for
30 minutes, or until the muffins are
golden and cooked through. Enjoy
warm or at room temperature.

COFFEE CHOCOLATE CHIP BANANA BREAD

Makes 10 to 12 slices

I've been making this banana bread recipe for my family for years now. I can't seem to keep a loaf of it around the house for more than a couple of hours after it emerges from the oven. As soon as I pull it out, hot and fresh with chocolate oozing, the kids come barreling in begging for slices. The ingredient that sets this loaf apart from other banana breads is the strong brewed coffee. Although most people wouldn't know it's in there, something special happens to the texture and flavor, making it a reliable family favorite we return to again and again.

3–4 ripe bananas (about 1 cup mashed)

⅓ cup butter, melted

½ cup granulated sugar

¼ cup firmly packed brown sugar

1 egg

1 teaspoon vanilla extract

¼ cup strong brewed coffee (see note)

1½ cups all-purpose flour

1 teaspoon baking soda

¼ teaspoon salt

½ cup chocolate chips

1 Preheat the oven to 350°F. Grease a 9" x 5" loaf pan.

2 Peel the bananas and add them to a mixing bowl. Roughly mash them with a potato masher, leaving some larger bite-size chunks. Stir in the butter, sugars, egg, vanilla, and coffee until combined. Add the flour, baking soda, and salt and stir until incorporated. Fold in the chocolate chips, reserving about 1 tablespoon to sprinkle on top. Spread the batter into the pan. Sprinkle the chocolate chips on top. Bake for 55 to 60 minutes, or until golden and cooked through. Cool on a wire rack for 20 minutes before running a butter knife around the edges of the pan and turning the loaf out. Serve warm or at room temperature.

NOTE: Decaffeinated coffee can be substituted if you prefer to cut back on the caffeine.

2 / SURVIVING ALASKA
SOUPS

SOUPS

*T*t was early October of 2011 when I pressed "publish" on my first post and officially became a food blogger. It was 40 degrees outside, the leaves were yellow, and it was raining. Celtic bagpipes were playing low on the speakers in the living room. I know this only because I made a commitment from the outset to begin most every blog post telling readers what the weather was like that day and what I was listening to as I cooked, photographed, and wrote. It was a window into my far-flung Alaska life—a means of inviting people in and a chance to virtually engage all of the senses the way sharing food together in person does.

When I was a young child, my grandmother had a record player tucked inside the little pantry in her Southern California kitchen. I didn't understand then that not everybody did this; it just seemed natural to me. It was then that I learned that food and music go together. Every kitchen has a rhythm, every cook a dance. I would don my miniature handmade apron and sit upon a step stool alongside a big semi-crystallized tin of honey (back when honey was kept in tins), a jar of yeast, canisters of poppy seeds and spices, a drippy vessel of molasses, and an old record player with a modest stack of vinyl records. They were Broadway musicals, mostly, like *Peter Pan,* one of Grandma's personal favorites. I had most of the words to the songs memorized, and with my hands firmly on my hips, I would sassily belt out, "I Won't Grow Up!" while she laughed and hummed along with me. Grandma always spoke very highly of the significance of a woman, Mary Martin, playing the starring role of Peter back in the 1950s. I realize now, looking back, that in addition to exposing me to culture and music and food, she was teaching me lessons in being a self-sufficient woman, a human being with a voice and an influence, who can step onto the world's stage and be absolutely anything I want to be. Today, when I turn on music in the kitchen, I feel empowered somehow and less isolated on this vast frontier.

Much like music, the seasons have always influenced what I'm making in the kitchen. I unashamedly posted three soup recipes in my first couple of months as a food blogger. I was experiencing my first transition from fall into winter in Alaska, and as the temperature plummeted and the snow began to fly, I was craving all things hot, hearty, and comforting.

It was still winter when we made the huge move from California to Alaska, in search of a slower pace of life. We sold most everything we had and stepped off the airplane with nothing more than two suitcases per family member. I knew I was starting life over in Alaska, from scratch. I didn't know a thing about snow cleats or studded tires or boot dryers, all Alaska winter necessities. I learned that it's very helpful to have a friend with a generator when the windstorms knock out your power for days on end, and to have another friend with a chain saw to take care of all the fallen trees after just such a windstorm. The water stops running when the power is out, I discovered, because the well pump requires power to get the water to the house. And my landlord suggested that I should trickle my faucets on the coldest nights so that the pipes don't freeze and burst in the dead of winter.

When we first arrived in Alaska in February, I found out the hard way that wind really can be biting and that sometimes you can legitimately choke on cold air. Upon arrival, I was surprised to discover that elementary-age students are sent out to recess at school down to -10°F. I had no idea the chore that it would be to bundle all three of the kids up in snow gear every morning before school and the even bigger chore it would be to keep track of six little gloves or three tiny hats along with snow pants, snow boots, scarves, and long underwear. With only a handful of hours of sunlight, it was dark when the kids left for school, and it was dark again when they came home. I found out very quickly what real cabin fever looks like and the need for vitamin D supplements.

THE CHANGEABLE WEATHER PATTERNS IN ALASKA CAN INFLUENCE EVERY BIT OF LIFE.

We lived quite a way outside of town. Four-wheel drive was a must. But even with four-wheel drive, many still get their vehicles stuck in a ditch, myself included. At that point, I needed to call up a friend with a truck and a tow strap. I had to learn how to navigate the roads when they are so packed with snow that none of the road lines are visible, guessing where lanes start and stop, or where parking spots are in parking lots. I discovered that it's often wiser not to slow down for a yellow light in winter because you'll slide straight on through the intersection. I now know how to pump my brakes on slick ice and how to attempt to avoid a moose when it darts into the road, as they so often do. I've learned that if you park your car at the airport for a few days during winter, you will return to a very dead battery. And I'm well acquainted with the sheer embarrassment of trying to push a shopping cart full of groceries to the car in the snow. The changeable weather patterns in Alaska can influence every bit of life. Of all the lessons that Alaska has taught me, perhaps the most important lesson of all is that I'm strong and capable and resilient, because you need to have a hardy measure of these things to survive this wild place.

Living here in one of the Earth's coldest climates, I've found that steaming pots of soup, long-braised stews, and stick-to-your-ribs chilis are among the most crave-worthy and essential recipes in my collection. I return to them again and again, and they become inexplicably familiar, like old friends or family heirlooms or music from childhood that you discover you still have memorized.

BLACK BEAN SOUP WITH REINDEER SAUSAGE AND SWEET POTATOES

Makes 4 to 6 servings

When I first wrote this recipe, I called it Black and Orange Soup because I made it for dinner on my children's first snowy Halloween in Alaska, just before we bundled up and went out trick-or-treating. The colors were appropriate for the occasion, and this filling pot of soup was just exactly what everyone needed before trudging out in the cold for buckets of candy.

If you don't have access to reindeer sausage, chicken, turkey, or beef smoked sausage are excellent alternatives.

1 tablespoon neutral-flavored oil, such as vegetable oil

1 pound reindeer smoked sausage or other smoked sausage, sliced

1 onion, chopped

3 cloves garlic, minced

8 ounces sweet potato, peeled and chopped

2 teaspoons chili powder

2 tablespoons ketchup

1 tablespoon Worcestershire sauce

¼ teaspoon liquid smoke (see note)

Salt and ground black pepper

1 can (14.5 ounces) chicken broth

1 can (14.5 ounces) fire-roasted diced tomatoes

4 cans (15 ounces each) black beans, rinsed and drained

½ cup cilantro, chopped

Juice of half a lime

FOR SERVING:

Sour cream

Corn chips

Cilantro, chopped

1 lime, sliced into wedges

1 In a Dutch oven or large pot, heat the oil over medium-high heat. Cook the smoked sausage until browned. Add the onion and cook for 2 minutes, or until tender. Add the garlic and cook for 1 minute.

2 Toss the sweet potato into the pot and add the chili powder, ketchup, Worcestershire sauce, liquid smoke, and salt and pepper to taste. Stir until the sausage and vegetables are coated with the seasonings.

3 Pour in the chicken broth, tomatoes, and black beans. Stir, cover, and reduce the heat to medium low. Simmer for 15 minutes, or until the sweet potato is tender.

4 Turn off the heat. Add the cilantro and lime juice. Taste for seasoning and add more salt as needed. Serve hot with sour cream, corn chips, and more chopped cilantro, with lime wedges on the side.

NOTE: Liquid smoke can often be found in a small bottle near the barbecue sauces or in the seasoning section of the baking aisle.

CAULIFLOWER CHOWDER SOURDOUGH BREAD BOWLS

Makes 4 servings

Cauliflower—a hardy Alaska grown vegetable—is showing up everywhere. It's a versatile option when making things like gluten free pizza crust, faux mashed potatoes, or cut finely and used as a stand-in for steamed rice. Here, I've made a creamy cauliflower chowder served up in a sourdough bread bowl, a new spin on the chowder bowls I devoured in college, sitting along the docks in San Diego.

½ pound bacon, chopped

¼ cup butter

1 onion, chopped

4 cloves garlic, chopped

2 carrots, chopped

2 ribs celery, chopped

Salt and freshly cracked black pepper

1 fresh bay leaf

¼ cup all-purpose flour

1 quart (4 cups) chicken broth

1 head cauliflower, cored and finely chopped

1 cup half-and-half

FOR SERVING:

4 small round loaves sourdough bread, tops sliced off and hollowed out

Smoked paprika

Cheddar cheese, grated

Green onions, sliced

1 In a large Dutch oven, cook the bacon over medium heat until browned and crisp. Remove the bacon to a plate lined with paper towels to cool and drain. Discard the bacon fat and return the pot to the heat.

2 Add the butter to the pot. Cook the onion and the garlic in the butter for 2 minutes. Add the carrots and celery. Season generously with salt and pepper to taste and add the bay leaf. Sprinkle the flour over the vegetables. Cook, stirring often, for 2 minutes. Add the chicken stock and stir well to combine, scraping the bottom of the pot as needed. Add the cauliflower and bring the soup to a boil. Reduce the heat and simmer, uncovered, stirring often, for 10 to 15 minutes, or until the vegetables are tender and the soup has thickened.

3 Turn off the heat and discard the bay leaf. Stir in the half-and-half. Add half of the bacon crumbles, reserving the other half for serving. The chowder should be thick. Season with more salt as needed and a generous amount of freshly cracked black pepper. Ladle the soup into the bread bowls and sprinkle each with a pinch of smoked paprika. Top each bread bowl with cheese, bacon, and green onions. Serve promptly.

TACO SOUP WITH GROUND TURKEY

Makes 6 servings

Sautéing chopped corn tortillas with the onion, jalapeño, and garlic thickens this soup and gives it a nice corn flavor throughout. Sprinkling crumbled corn tortilla chips on top is the perfect way to complete the taco flavor and add some nice crunch. Top the soup as you would a taco—with grated cheese, sour cream, and avocado.

2 tablespoons avocado oil

1 onion, chopped

1 jalapeño chile pepper, finely chopped

2 cloves garlic, minced

1/3 cup cilantro, chopped

6 yellow corn tortillas, chopped

1 1/2 tablespoons chili powder

1 tablespoon ground cumin

1/2 teaspoon ground chipotle chile pepper

1 teaspoon garlic powder

1 teaspoon salt

1 1/2 pounds ground turkey

1 can (15 ounces) pinto beans, rinsed and drained

1 can (14.5 ounces) diced tomatoes

1 quart (4 cups) chicken broth

1 cup corn

FOR SERVING:

Cheddar cheese, grated

Corn chips, crushed

Cilantro, chopped

Sour cream

Avocado, pitted, peeled, and sliced

In a Dutch oven or large pot, heat the avocado oil over medium heat. Add the onion, jalapeño pepper, garlic, cilantro, and corn tortillas. Cook, stirring frequently, until the onion becomes tender. Stir in the chili powder, cumin, chipotle pepper, garlic powder, and salt. Allow the spices to toast, stirring often, for 90 seconds. Add the turkey and cook until browned. Pour in the pinto beans, tomatoes, and chicken broth. Bring the soup to a simmer. Stir in the corn and heat through. Ladle the soup into bowls and serve with cheese, corn chips, cilantro, sour cream, and avocado slices.

CURRIED CHICKEN AND RICE SOUP WITH APPLES

Makes 4 servings

This is my version of Indian mulligatawny soup, and it's been a well-reviewed recipe on my blog and in my weekly food column in the newspaper. This colorful, fragrant soup comes together quickly. The subtle sweetness of the apples and the warmth of the curry make this a perfect fall into winter weeknight meal. This is also a great one to make when you have leftover roasted or rotisserie chicken on hand. Rather than using uncooked chicken as called for in the recipe, just shred up your leftover cooked chicken and stir it in as a substitute for the chopped chicken.

3 tablespoons butter

2 carrots, chopped

2 ribs celery, chopped

1/2 large onion, chopped

1 apple, peeled and chopped

2 teaspoons curry powder

3 tablespoons all-purpose flour

1 pound boneless, skinless chicken, chopped

1 quart (4 cups) chicken broth

1/3 cup jasmine rice

1/4 cup half-and-half (or coconut milk)

Salt and ground black pepper

1 In a Dutch oven, melt the butter over medium heat. Cook the carrots, celery, and onion, stirring frequently, for 2 minutes. Add the apple and sprinkle in the curry powder. Stir to coat, cooking for 2 minutes, or until the curry is toasted and fragrant. Add the flour to the pot, stirring to combine, and cook for 2 minutes.

2 Add the chicken, chicken broth, and rice to the pot. Bring to a boil, reduce the heat to medium low, and simmer for 20 minutes, stirring occasionally to prevent the rice from sticking to the bottom of the pot, or until the chicken and rice are cooked through.

3 Remove the pot from the heat and stir in the half-and-half. Season with salt and pepper to taste. Ladle into bowls and serve.

ROASTED TOMATO SOUP

Makes 4 servings

If I present my oldest son, Brady, with a perfectly melty and golden grilled cheese sandwich, he will immediately ask, "Where's the tomato soup?" If there isn't any tomato soup to be had for sandwich dipping and subsequent slurping, he will be thoroughly disappointed with life. I've learned that it's best to keep a fail-proof, delicious tomato soup recipe on hand for all such grilled cheese sandwich occasions, which at our house are about once every other week. It's one of our favorite meals.

I've found that I prefer tomato soup recipes that stray far away from garlic and Italian herbs, as that inevitably causes them to taste like a bowl of marinara sauce to me. This is my favorite version. I lightly adapted it from Homemade with Love by Jennifer Perillo. Before reading this recipe in her beautifully inviting cookbook, I had never tried roasting canned tomatoes. It was a complete revelation to me, and a necessary one, as tomatoes don't grow well in Alaska without some serious gardening skills and a greenhouse, of which I have neither. Canned tomatoes are a pantry staple here on the Last Frontier. Roasting them, as Jennifer recommends, elevates them and removes that tinny flavor you often find. Plus, the addition of brown sugar and ground cloves gives the soup a long-simmered warmth. You'd never know how easy it is and how quickly it comes together once the tomatoes finish roasting.

recipe continues

1 can (28 ounces) whole tomatoes

1 tablespoon brown sugar

½ teaspoon kosher salt

¼ teaspoon ground black pepper

¼ teaspoon ground cloves

¼ teaspoon red-pepper flakes

2 tablespoons extra-virgin olive oil

1 cup vegetable broth

1 cup heavy cream

1 Preheat the oven to 300°F.

2 Drain the tomatoes, reserving all of the liquid. Slice the tomatoes in half length-wise. Place them cut side up onto a large rimmed baking sheet.

3 In a small bowl, stir together the brown sugar, salt, black pepper, cloves, and red-pepper flakes. Sprinkle the mixture evenly over the tomatoes. Drizzle the tomatoes with the olive oil. Roast the tomatoes for 1 hour.

4 Transfer the roasted tomatoes and all of the pan juices to a blender along with the vegetable broth and all of the reserved liquid. Whirl until smooth. Transfer the soup to a saucepan and place over medium-high heat. Heat, stirring often, until steaming hot, but not boiling. Turn off the heat and stir in the cream. Taste for seasoning and add additional salt if needed. Serve promptly.

SPICY CHORIZO RED LENTIL SOUP WITH KALE

Makes 6 to 8 servings

This is just the sort of meaty, vegetable-laden, stick-to-your-ribs meal I dream about to help get me through the long, dark Alaska winters. Mexican chorizo gives this soup its deep red color and a complex heat that warms you down to your bones. The lentils are hearty and inviting, thickening the entire pot and offering extra protein. Be sure to have plenty of crusty bread on hand to tear off in big hunks and dip directly into your bowl. This recipe makes a fair amount and makes great leftovers. Note: This spicy chorizo soup is such a perfect Alaska meal that we chose to feature it on the cover!

1 pound ground Mexican-style chorizo

1 onion, chopped

2 cloves garlic, minced

2 carrots, chopped

2 ribs celery, chopped

2 cups chopped kale

Salt and freshly cracked black pepper

1 cup red lentils

1 can (14.5 ounces) diced tomatoes, undrained

2 quarts (8 cups) chicken broth

In a large pot or Dutch oven, brown the chorizo over medium-high heat. Add the onion, garlic, carrots, celery, and kale and cook, stirring often, for 5 minutes, or until the vegetables start to become tender. Season with salt and pepper. Add the lentils, tomatoes, and chicken broth and bring to a boil. Reduce the heat to low, cover, and simmer, stirring often, for 20 minutes, or until the lentils are soft. When the lentils are soft and the soup has thickened, taste for seasoning. Add more salt and pepper as needed. Serve with crusty bread. Leftovers keep well in the refrigerator for up to 7 days. This soup also freezes well.

ASIAN CHICKEN NOODLE SOUP WITH SHIITAKE MUSHROOMS

Makes 6 servings

Now this is a chicken noodle soup recipe I can get behind. Reconstituting the dried shiitakes directly in the soup allows you to capitalize on all that deep, earthy mushroom flavor, making the broth a captivating dark brown, swirling with umami. I like to add a little extra heat to mine at the table in the form of sambal oelek, an Indonesian chili paste that can be found in the Asian section of most markets, often near the Sriracha. I enjoy my noodles, chicken, and vegetables with chopsticks before picking up my bowl without shame and drinking the broth.

FOR THE CHICKEN THIGHS:

1½ pounds boneless, skinless chicken thighs

1 tablespoon Chinese 5-spice powder

½ teaspoon kosher salt

¼ teaspoon freshly cracked black pepper

1 tablespoon vegetable oil

FOR THE SOUP:

3 cloves garlic, minced

1 tablespoon grated fresh ginger

1 teaspoon sambal oelek

1 pound baby bok choy, sliced

1 cup dried shiitake mushrooms

1½ quarts (6 cups) chicken broth

2 tablespoons soy sauce

1 teaspoon sugar

1 tablespoon toasted sesame oil

4 ounces thin rice noodles

FOR SERVING:

Green onions, sliced

Sriracha or additional sambal oelek

1 *To make the chicken thighs:* Pat the chicken thighs dry. In a small bowl, stir together the 5-spice powder, salt, and pepper. Sprinkle both sides of the chicken thighs with the spice mixture. In a Dutch oven, heat the vegetable oil over medium heat. Cook the chicken thighs for 8 to 10 minutes, turning once, or until seared on both sides and a thermometer inserted in the thickest portion registers 165°F. Transfer the thighs to a plate to rest, reserving the oil and juices in the pot. Cover the plate to keep warm.

2 *To make the soup:* Add the garlic, ginger, and sambal oelek to the pot and cook, stirring frequently, for 1 minute. Add the bok choy and mushrooms to the pot. Cover with the chicken broth. Stir in the soy sauce, sugar, and sesame oil. Bring the soup to a boil, reduce the heat to medium low, and simmer for 10 minutes, or until the bok choy and mushrooms are tender. Add the noodles to the pot, stir, and remove the pot from the heat. Let the noodles sit in the hot broth for 3 to 4 minutes, or until tender. Meanwhile, slice the chicken thighs. Serve the soup in bowls with the sliced chicken thighs and green onions on top and sambal oelek or Sriracha on the side.

WHITE BEAN SOUP WITH SPINACH AND ITALIAN SAUSAGE

Makes 4 to 6 servings

This is by far the fastest and easiest soup in the book, taking less than 30 minutes from start to finish. Italian sausage is one of the best ways to bring a lot of flavor to a dish in a short period of time, which is why I turn to it again and again when making a speedy tomato meat sauce for pasta or a quick pot of soup. This is an ideal weeknight meal at the end of a busy day, when you want to get something warm, cozy, and homemade on the table in no time flat. This creamy yet brothy soup is perfect for dipping a nice loaf of crusty bread. Add more red-pepper flakes at the table if you want a little more heat, like I do.

1 tablespoon extra-virgin olive oil

¼ teaspoon red-pepper flakes

1 pound bulk mild Italian sausage

1 onion, chopped

3 cloves garlic, minced

2 cans (15 ounces each) white beans, rinsed and drained

1 quart (4 cups) chicken broth

¾ cup heavy cream

5 ounces baby spinach, chopped

Salt and freshly cracked black pepper

In a Dutch oven, heat the oil and red-pepper flakes over medium heat. Cook the sausage until browned. Add the onion and garlic and cook for 2 minutes, or until tender and fragrant. Pour in the white beans, followed by the chicken broth. Bring to a simmer to heat through. Turn off the heat. Stir in the cream and spinach. Season to taste with salt and black pepper. Serve promptly with crusty bread.

MOOSE CHILI

Makes 6 servings

My favorite way to introduce out-of-town guests to eating moose is with a familiar, flavorful pot of chili. Moose is often readily available here in Alaska, and when ground, its subtle flavor makes a perfect substitute for lean ground beef. It's not at all gamey like venison, as most people expect. However, if you don't have access to moose, I've made similar versions of this chili over the years with ground beef and ground turkey as well, so feel free to try it with what you have on hand. Don't skip the avocado on top. It adds the perfect cooling creaminess against the smoky heat of the chipotle. Serve with freshly baked cornbread or corn chips on the side.

1½ pounds ground moose or ground beef

1 red onion, chopped

2 tablespoons chili powder

1 tablespoon ground cumin

1 teaspoon salt

1 canned chipotle in adobo sauce, finely chopped

2 tablespoons tomato paste

2 cans (15 ounces each) black beans, rinsed and drained

1 can (15 ounces) dark red kidney beans, rinsed and drained

1 can (14.4 ounces) diced tomatoes

1 can (15 ounces) beef broth

Juice of half a lime

FOR SERVING:

Jack cheese, grated

1 ripe avocado, pitted, peeled, and chopped

Red onion, finely chopped

Cilantro, chopped

1 In a Dutch oven, brown the moose meat or beef over medium heat. Add the onion and cook for 2 minutes, or until tender. Stir in the chili powder, cumin, salt, chipotle, and tomato paste. Pour in the beans, tomatoes, and beef broth, stirring to combine. Bring the mixture to a simmer, reduce the heat to low, and cook, uncovered, for 60 minutes, stirring often to prevent sticking. The chili will thicken as it cooks. Remove from the heat and stir in the lime juice.

2 To serve, ladle the chili into bowls. Top with cheese, avocado, onion, and cilantro. Corn chips or cornbread recommended on the side.

3/ BOUNTIFUL ALASKA SEAFOOD

SEAFOOD

*T*he Kenai Peninsula is nothing if not a fishing community. We are surrounded by the pristine waters of Cook Inlet, Kachemak and Resurrection Bays, Prince William Sound, and the Gulf of Alaska. Not to mention countless lakes and formidable rivers, like the world-famous Kenai River. Alaska's waters are home to some of the most stunning and delicious wild seafood in the world— crab à la *Deadliest Catch,* ginormous halibut, succulent oysters, sweet spot prawns, sexy razor clams, massive weathervane scallops, decadent black cod, all the gorgeous salmon you could ever dream of, and so much more.

When fishing season hits, our peninsula that had been hibernating through the long winter suddenly comes alive and takes on a new rhythm, bustling with energy. Optimism abounds like wildflowers on the roadside. Folks in the street chatter about everything from sport fishing to commercial fishing to subsistence fishing. Many come from the Lower 48 hoping for the catch of a lifetime. Others come to fill their freezers to feed their families and survive the next long, dark Alaska winter. Businesses reopen, and the roads fill with motor homes and pickup trucks with huge fishing nets adorning their beds. Restaurants and stores and campgrounds overflow. Our quiet towns become full of activity into the late hours of the night, thanks to the midnight sun. The brown bears become active again and are drawn to the waters, looking for their summer feast, sometimes lumbering across the road, stopping traffic in Cooper Landing. Even the birds flock to the peninsula, migrating in for the season, circling over the shores and calling so loudly that they can be heard from miles away. Boat engines groaning, waves crashing, gulls calling . . . all the distinct sounds of fishing season.

It was right at the beginning of the busy tourist season that I spotted a summer opening for a line cook at The Flats Bistro, the finest restaurant in town. Being a fan of the restaurant and needing some extra income, I applied on a whim. Although I am a food writer, I had only ever worked in one tiny café briefly when just out of college many years ago, and I had basically little to no experience in a big professional kitchen. Most everything I knew about working in restaurants, I had learned from watching professional chefs on TV. I wasn't sure that my self-taught home cooking and food blogging skills would translate across to a hectic dinner service in a popular restaurant during the busiest season of the year.

When I went in for the interview, the head chef at the time asked me what I was most comfortable cooking off their dinner menu.

"Seafood," I replied. Seafood I knew I could do.

The next thing I knew, I was asked to come in for a shift. I pulled my hair back in a messy bun, selected one of my colorful bandanas, and tied it around my head, a style that soon became my trademark at the restaurant. I snapped on a black collared kitchen shirt, the first I'd ever worn. I washed my hands, grabbed my chef's knife that I had brought from home, and took a quick glance at myself in the mirror, realizing just momentarily that I suddenly looked like a chef, but refusing to let it sink in.

I entered the kitchen, and immediately my senses were overwhelmed with frenetic clamor and noise—loud fans whirring, the dishwasher splashing, dishes clanking, pots banging, the rhythmic sound of knives chopping on cutting boards, tickets printing orders, servers shouting, the radio blasting alternative rock music, potatoes boiling, ovens slamming shut, cooks reading tickets and calling out orders . . . *"Hot food!"* . . . *"Order up!"* . . . *"Pans!"* While at first it was all just noise mixed with choice expletives, I soon discovered that it was like a foreign language that I needed to decipher. I needed to hear all these distinct sounds, understand them, make sense of them, and contribute to them, finding my place somewhere in it all, cussing included. *"Firing the fish . . . Four minutes out . . . Where the hell is the damn remoulade?!"*

A restaurant kitchen during dinner service is a dynamic, exhilarating place, constantly in motion, never stopping. My first day was a whirlwind. I went home from training covered in food and grease, aching all over, my mind spinning like a top, and cried myself to sleep from exhaustion and being utterly overwhelmed. The next day, when I arrived, I was surprised to discover that I had been given my own station. I had been thrown straight into deep waters, swimming against the tide. Someone clearly thought I could do it, but I wasn't yet convinced. I knew how to execute beautiful food at home with my own recipes at my own pace. But what I had to learn was how to consistently make

I HAD BEEN THROWN STRAIGHT INTO DEEP WATERS, SWIMMING AGAINST THE TIDE.

many different dishes of someone else's food as quickly as humanly possible, while still making them beautiful. To work in a professional kitchen, I had to learn once again to find my voice, to be heard above the clamor, to bust my ass and hustle, to stand my ground as a tiny 5-foot-1 woman in a male-dominated profession. I knew I had arrived when, after I had been working there a few days, the grill cook, Derik, passed me a hot sizzle plate with six plump shrimp for the salad I was plating and said with a smile, "You move like you've been in a kitchen before."

Indeed. Indeed, I have.

On my station, I made all of the salads, did some of the appetizers, and plated the desserts. Most importantly, I made the fish and chips, razor clams, and oysters straight out of Kachemak Bay. Prior to working at the restaurant, I had never shucked an oyster in my life. There's nothing like having to shuck dozens of oysters quickly and perfectly while tickets mound up on your board overflowing with other orders you're neglecting to give you a quick crash course on oyster shucking. When a ticket for oysters would come in, I'd groan because everything else I was doing had to come to a grinding halt while I tackled the stubborn, intimidating, sharp-edged little suckers. I sliced my fingers wide open on more than one occasion on those damn things. Sometimes when we were slammed with customers, the dish washer, other line cooks, or even the owner would step in to help shuck oysters. One memorable night, I had a customer order more than 100 oysters during a single dinner service because he was enjoying them so immensely. By the end of the evening, the customer requested to compliment the chef who had done the shucking. I felt like a real badass that night, a true oyster expert at last. Sometimes I even miss shucking those pesky things.

By August, the restaurant asked me to stay on staff at the end of the season, and I began developing nightly seafood specials and other items for the menu. Besides the lovely Mariah who worked in the dish pit, I was the only woman left in the kitchen during dinner services that summer—and I had the knife skills, burn marks, and vocabulary to prove it. By fall, the owner asked me to manage a brand-new Sunday brunch service, with a menu all my own. It wasn't until then that I felt I could actually consider calling myself a chef. Somehow, somewhere along the way—between razor clams and oyster shucking, between fish and chips and king crab eggs Benedict—this self-taught home cook and food writer became something more.

KING CRAB AVOCADO TOAST

Makes 2 servings

I don't love avocados because they're trendy to put on toast. I fell in love with avocados as a child when my grandma Susan had a massive avocado tree in her yard in Southern California. From the tree dangled a rope swing where I would sway my days away in the shade. The avocados were so abundant that they would overripen and fall to the ground, their dark cobbled shells bursting open to reveal the bright green inside. I would snack on them often. As I grew up and became a cook, avocados have always been there in my food, a reflection of my roots at the base of that California avocado tree.

Avocados can't grow in Alaska, so they are a bit of a luxury up here. Perfectly ripe fruit that hasn't been bruised and damaged by thousands of miles of travel can be hard to come by, and we pay a premium for them. So if I'm going to splurge and put half of an avocado on my toast, I might as well go all out and top it with succulent Alaska king crab: marrying two of my worlds on one beautiful, decadent plate. I season my avocado and crab simply with lemon, salt, and chives to really allow the natural flavors of the avocado and crab to shine.

1 ripe avocado

1 lemon, cut into wedges

Salt

2 slices French bread, toasted

½ cup Alaska king crab meat

1 tablespoon chopped fresh chives

1 Halve the avocado and remove the pit. Scoop the flesh from the shell into a bowl. Mash the avocado thoroughly with a fork. Squeeze 2 teaspoons of juice from a lemon wedge and add to the avocado. Season with salt to taste, stirring to combine. Spread the avocado onto the toast.

2 Add the crab meat to a bowl. Squeeze a lemon wedge over top of the crab, stirring to coat. Season with salt to taste. Divide the crab evenly between both slices of toast. Sprinkle the crab with the chives. Serve with lemon wedges on the side.

BLACK COD OVER UDON WITH BABY BOK CHOY

——— *Makes 2 servings* ———

Black cod is like the pork belly or bone marrow of the ocean, deeply rich and decadent. Because of its unctuous nature, it goes well with this vinegar-forward umami broth and some tender-crisp bok choy. One trick about preparing black cod is that the bones are notoriously difficult to remove; it's best to attempt to tackle the bones after the fish has been cooked.

FOR THE UDON:
8 ounces udon noodles
1 cup vegetable broth
¼ cup soy sauce
¼ cup seasoned rice vinegar
1 tablespoon honey
1 tablespoon finely chopped fresh ginger

1 clove garlic, minced
1 green onion, sliced thickly on the bias

FOR THE BLACK COD:
2 tablespoons hoisin
1 teaspoon sambal oelek
2 teaspoons vegetable oil

2 fillets (4–5 ounces each) Alaska black cod

FOR THE BOK CHOY:
2 teaspoons toasted sesame oil
2 baby bok choy, sliced in half
1 teaspoon sugar
Kosher salt

1 Preheat the oven to 450°F.

2 *To make the udon:* Prepare the udon noodles according to package directions. Meanwhile, in a small saucepan over medium-low heat, stir together the vegetable broth, soy sauce, vinegar, honey, ginger, and garlic. Bring to a simmer. Keep the broth warm while completing the other steps.

3 *To make the black cod:* In a small bowl, stir together the hoisin and sambal oelek. Set aside. In an ovenproof skillet, heat the vegetable oil over medium-high heat. When the oil is hot, add the black cod fillets skin side up and sear for 2 minutes, or until golden brown on the bottom. Carefully turn the fillets. Turn off the heat. Using a spoon, spread the hoisin mixture over the top of each fillet. Transfer the pan to the oven and roast the fillets for 5 minutes.

4 *To make the bok choy:* While the fish is in the oven, in a skillet, heat the sesame oil over medium-high heat. Sprinkle the cut side of the bok choy with the sugar. Place them cut side down into the hot sesame oil. Cover and sear for 2 minutes, or until caramelized. Turn the bok choy over and add ¼ cup water to the pan. Cover and allow the bok choy to steam for 3 minutes. Season with salt to taste.

5 Debone the fish with fish tweezers or using your fingers.

6 To assemble the dish, divide the cooked udon between 2 bowls. Pour half of the hot broth mixture over each bowl of udon. Top each with a fillet of black cod and 2 halves of bok choy. Sprinkle with green onions and serve.

BLACKENED SALMON LETTUCE WRAPS WITH MANGO SALSA AND AVOCADO CREAM

Makes 4 servings

I originally got the recipe for the salmon spice rub in this dish from my friend and fellow Alaskan Heidi Drygas, from her blog Chena Girl Cooks. And she adapted the recipe from the Alaska Seafood Marketing Institute. This smoky-sweet spice rub pairs perfectly with a robust, lean sockeye salmon. I've been using the rub for years in many different preparations, and I even served it on a seafood entrée special when I worked at the bistro because we had fresh sockeye in house. It completely sold out.

This version with blackened salmon tucked into a crisp lettuce wrap and topped with refreshing mango salsa and cooling avocado cream is another winner. I couldn't stop eating them as I was testing this recipe, because in addition to being downright delicious, they are also incredibly healthy, full of fresh fruit, vegetables, and lean protein.

FOR THE MANGO SALSA:
1 ripe mango, finely cubed
1 red bell pepper, chopped
1/2 cup chopped red onion
1 jalapeño chile pepper, seeded and finely chopped
1/3 cup cilantro, chopped
Juice of half a lime
Salt

FOR THE AVOCADO CREAM:
1 ripe avocado, pitted and peeled
1 clove garlic
1/4 cup cilantro
Juice of half a lime
1/3 cup sour cream
Milk, for thinning
Salt

FOR THE BLACKENED SALMON:
2 tablespoons sugar
1 tablespoon chili powder
1 1/2 teaspoons smoked paprika
1 1/2 teaspoons ground cumin
1 1/2 teaspoons kosher salt
1 teaspoon ground black pepper
1/4 teaspoon dry mustard
Pinch of cinnamon
4 fillets (4–6 ounces each) wild Alaska sockeye salmon, pin bones removed
1 tablespoon avocado oil

FOR SERVING:
1 head butter lettuce, separated into individual leaves

recipe continues

1 *To make the mango salsa:* In a medium bowl, fold together the mango, bell pepper, onion, jalapeño pepper, cilantro, and lime juice. Season with salt to taste. Refrigerate while you complete the next steps.

2 *To make the avocado cream:* In a food processor, combine the avocado, garlic, cilantro, lime juice, and sour cream. Process, drizzling milk in gradually until the avocado cream is smooth and spreadable. Season with salt to taste.

3 *To make the blackened salmon:* In a small bowl, stir together the sugar, chili powder, paprika, cumin, salt, black pepper, mustard, and cinnamon. Generously coat the top of each salmon fillet with the spice rub, pressing it down gently into the fish to adhere.

4 In a large skillet, heat the avocado oil over medium-high heat. Once the oil is hot, carefully place the fillets sea-soning side down into the oil, pressing down on the fillets to ensure that all of the fillet is making direct contact with the pan. To protect from oil splatters, cover the pan with a lid. Sear the salmon for 2 to 3 minutes, or until caramelized on the bottom. Turn the salmon and cook, skin side down, for 2 to 3 minutes, or until medium-rare to medium in the center. Remove the pan from the heat and allow the salmon to rest for 3 minutes before removing the skin. The skin should peel away easily from the fillet.

5 *To assemble the lettuce wraps:* Using a fork or your fingers, flake the blackened salmon roughly in large chunks. Place a small handful of salmon flakes onto each lettuce cup. Top each lettuce cup with a generous spoon of mango salsa. Serve with avocado cream on the side.

SALMON BURGERS WITH SESAME SLAW AND WASABI MAYO

Makes 4

Salmon burgers are very Alaska. You can find variations of them in restaurants and homes statewide. They are at the top of the list of my favorite ways to enjoy and serve local sockeye salmon, a real crowd pleaser to make for guests. Even fish-averse kiddos tend to enjoy salmon when it comes in burger form. I admit I may even enjoy a good salmon burger more than a traditional hamburger. Gasp.

While a great many salmon burger recipes call for leftover salmon that's already been cooked and flaked, mixed with bread crumbs as a binder, I prefer to make my burgers with raw cubed salmon and panko. This method produces a beautiful, moist patty that really lets the salmon stand out. Once you've got this method down, you can play with different toppings. They are fantastic with classic burger fixin's like red onion, tomato, and lettuce with a garlicky lemon mayonnaise or homemade tartar sauce. Or, in this version, I evoked the flavors of sushi—ginger, sesame, Sriracha, avocado, and wasabi. As with a salmon fillet, salmon burgers are enjoyed best medium-rare to medium in the center.

FOR THE SESAME SLAW:

¼ cup rice wine vinegar

3 tablespoons sesame oil

2 teaspoons Sriracha

2 teaspoons sugar

Juice of half a lime

2 teaspoons toasted sesame seeds

¼ teaspoon salt

2 cups finely shredded red cabbage

⅓ cup cilantro, chopped

FOR THE WASABI MAYO:

⅓ cup mayonnaise

1 tablespoon wasabi paste (or to taste)

1 teaspoon soy sauce

FOR THE SALMON BURGERS:

2 pounds wild sockeye salmon, pin bones and skin removed, cubed

¾ cup panko bread crumbs

⅓ cup thinly sliced green onions

1 teaspoon grated fresh ginger

1 clove garlic, minced

2 egg whites

3 tablespoons soy sauce

Juice of half a lime

½ teaspoon salt

2 tablespoons avocado oil

4 hamburger buns, toasted

1 ripe avocado, sliced

recipe continues

1 *To make the sesame slaw:* In a mixing bowl, combine the vinegar, sesame oil, Sriracha, sugar, lime juice, sesame seeds, and salt. Whisk vigorously to thoroughly combine and dissolve sugar. Add the cabbage and cilantro and toss to coat. Refrigerate until ready to assemble the burgers. I do not recommend making this more than an hour ahead, as the cabbage will begin to wilt and lose its crunch.

2 *To make the wasabi mayo:* In a small bowl, stir together the mayonnaise, wasabi, and soy sauce until smooth. Cover and refrigerate until ready to serve.

3 *To make the salmon burgers:* In a mixing bowl, combine the salmon, panko, green onions, ginger, garlic, egg whites, soy sauce, lime juice, and salt. Fold together until well combined. On a large cutting board, shape the mixture into 4 evenly sized round patties.

4 Place a large nonstick skillet over medium-high heat. Swirl the pan with the avocado oil. When the oil is hot, carefully transfer 2 salmon burgers to the pan. Cook for 2 to 3 minutes, or until seared and browned on the bottom. Turn and cook for 2 to 3 minutes, or until seared on the other side. Remove the burgers from the heat and repeat with the remaining patties.

5 Place the toasted burger buns on serving plates. Place a salmon burger on each bottom bun. Using a slotted spoon, top each burger with a generous heap of sesame slaw. Top the slaw with avocado slices. Smear each top bun liberally with wasabi mayo and place them on top of the burgers. Serve promptly.

SEARED HALIBUT PASTA WITH PISTACHIO PESTO AND ROASTED TOMATOES

Makes 4 servings

At the very tip of the Kenai Peninsula is Homer, Alaska: the halibut fishing capital of the world. A day of fishing can sometimes yield massive halibut weighing hundreds of pounds. Halibut have a mild flavor but are sturdy and meaty in texture. The main thing to know about cooking halibut is that you absolutely do not want to overcook it, especially if you've worked so hard to catch it or spent a pretty penny on it at the fish monger. At medium-rare to medium, the center of the fish is glistening and almost opalescent, perfect to eat. Beyond that, halibut dries out rapidly and is much less enjoyable. Because of its tendency to dry out, I like a quick hard sear, as in this recipe, or a delicate poach, as you'll see later in the chapter. For searing your halibut, it's handy to own a metal fish spatula to help get up under the fish without damaging the fillet.

FOR THE ROASTED TOMATOES:

2 cups small yellow and red tomatoes, such as grape and cherry, sliced in half

2 tablespoons extra-virgin olive oil

Sea salt

Freshly ground black pepper

FOR THE PISTACHIO PESTO:

1 cup shelled roasted pistachios

1 cup basil leaves

¼ cup cilantro

2 cloves garlic

Zest of 1 lemon

3 tablespoons grated Parmesan cheese

½ cup extra-virgin olive oil, divided

Kosher salt

16 ounces angel-hair pasta

1 tablespoon avocado oil

4 fillets (4–6 ounces) halibut

Sea salt and freshly ground black pepper

recipe continues

1 *To make the roasted tomatoes:* Preheat the oven to 400°F. Line a rimmed baking sheet with foil. Arrange the tomatoes on the pan. Drizzle the tomatoes with the olive oil and season generously with salt and pepper. Roast for 15 to 20 minutes, or until softened and blistered.

2 *To make the pistachio pesto:* Meanwhile, in a food processor, combine the pistachios, basil, cilantro, garlic, lemon zest, cheese, and ¼ cup of the olive oil. Process on medium speed, drizzling in more olive oil as needed to reach the desired consistency. The pesto should be slightly thinner than a paste, but not runny. Season with kosher salt to taste.

3 Prepare the pasta according to package directions for al dente. Drain lightly, reserving about ¼ cup of the pasta water. Return the angel hair to the pot with the pasta water. Stir in the pesto until coated.

4 In a cast-iron skillet, heat the avocado oil over medium-high heat. Pat the halibut fillets dry and season them with salt and pepper to taste. Sear them until browned on the bottom, about 4 minutes (see note). Gently turn them with a metal fish spatula and cook for 60 to 90 seconds, or until cooked to medium-rare to medium in the center, being careful not to overcook, or they will become dry.

5 *To plate the pasta:* Divide the pesto-coated angel hair among 4 pasta bowls. Top each bowl of pasta with a halibut fillet. Distribute the roasted tomatoes evenly among the 4 bowls. Serve promptly with freshly grated Parmesan.

NOTE: Searing time will vary depending on the thickness of your fillets. If your fillets are quite thick, the cast-iron skillet can be transferred to a 350°F oven to finish cooking. But again, be very careful not to overcook and dry out the halibut.

SLOW-ROASTED KING SALMON WITH CUCUMBER DILL SAUCE

Makes 6 to 8 servings

A few years back we celebrated my grandmother's 80th birthday at my aunt and uncle's beautiful property in California. When I offered to help in the kitchen to prepare the Wilson family feast, my aunt Claudette showed me the most stunning fillet of king salmon they had purchased from their fish monger in San Diego. She placed it in the oven on a very low temperature to slow roast. She then handed me a recipe for cucumber sauce written by Julia Child and asked me to make a version of it to accompany the salmon. I quickly went to work peeling and deseeding cucumbers while my aunt stood alongside me making her trademark vinaigrette.

When the meal was ready, we took it outside to a long table, where the warm sun was casting tall golden streams through the canopy of massive oak trees above. We ate family style, my aunt portioning pieces of salmon alongside a perfectly dressed crisp green salad. The cucumber sauce was passed around as my uncle poured the iced tea. Laughter and memories were plentiful, and the meal will never be forgotten. I took a copy of the cucumber sauce recipe home and have kept it all this time, waiting for an opportunity to write about it.

When you're fortunate enough to have a side of wild king salmon grace your kitchen, slow roasting is a perfect option. King salmon has a milder flavor and higher fat content than sockeye, so it works beautifully with a gentler preparation and more subtle flavor profiles. As the fillet roasts at a low temperature, the fat melts ever so slowly, making the delicate meat incredibly succulent. The cooling cucumber dill sauce truly allows the king salmon to shine.

recipe continues

1 side (2.5 pounds) wild king salmon, pin bones removed

Extra-virgin olive oil

Sea salt

Freshly cracked black pepper

FOR THE CUCUMBER DILL SAUCE:

1 English cucumber, peeled, seeds removed, and chopped

2 tablespoons fresh dill, finely chopped

1 cup sour cream

1/2 teaspoon kosher salt

1/2 teaspoon sugar

1 teaspoon white wine vinegar

FOR SERVING:

Lightly dressed green salad (I recommend a subtle lemon and olive oil vinaigrette)

1 lemon, cut into wedges

1 Place a pan of warm water on the bottom rack in the oven. Place the upper rack in the center position. Preheat the oven to 200°F. Line a large rimmed baking sheet with foil, then grease the foil with olive oil. Place the whole side of salmon onto the foil skin side down. Lightly coat the top of the salmon with more olive oil and season generously with sea salt and pepper. Place the pan in the oven on the upper rack and roast the salmon for 45 minutes.

2 *To make the cucumber dill sauce:* Meanwhile, in a bowl, stir together the cucumber, dill, sour cream, salt, sugar, and vinegar. Cover and refrigerate until ready to serve.

3 Check the salmon for doneness; roasting time will depend on the thickness of the fillet. The salmon should be just barely firm when touched, and still pink and moist in the center for medium-rare to medium. If not done, return it to the oven for 10 minutes and check again. When done, remove the salmon from the oven and allow to rest for 10 minutes.

4 To serve, break off large chunks of salmon, using forks (the meat will slide away easily from the skin on the bottom). Serve warm with the cucumber dill sauce and a lightly dressed green salad. Lemon wedges and sea salt on the side.

SALMON SUPERFOOD SALAD

Makes 2 servings

This salad is so stunning and delicious you don't even realize how insanely healthy it is. It's packed with 5 designated super foods that are considered to be especially beneficial for health and well-being: leafy green kale, protein-rich quinoa, creamy avocado, lean sockeye salmon, and pomegranate arils. I top it all with an irresistible honey-mustard vinaigrette. Tip: Give your kale a good firm massage for 30 seconds to tenderize it and help it turn a more vibrant green.

2 fillets (4 ounces each) wild Alaska sockeye salmon, pin bones and skin removed

Salt and freshly cracked black pepper

½ tablespoon avocado oil

FOR THE HONEY-MUSTARD VINAIGRETTE:

½ cup extra-virgin olive oil

3 tablespoons white wine vinegar

1½ tablespoons honey

1 tablespoon Dijon mustard

1 large clove garlic, minced

Salt and freshly cracked black pepper

3 cups finely chopped kale

1 cup cooked quinoa, cooled

1 ripe avocado, pitted, peeled, and chopped

½ cup pomegranate arils

1 Season the salmon fillets with salt and pepper to taste. In a skillet, heat the oil over medium-high heat and sear the fillets until golden and cooked to your liking on both sides. (I like mine medium, which takes only 4 to 6 minutes, turning once.) Set aside and allow to rest.

2 *To make the honey-mustard vinaigrette:* In a food processor, combine the oil, vinegar, honey, mustard, garlic, and salt and pepper to taste. Process for 30 seconds, or until smooth and emulsified. Set aside.

3 Add the kale to a bowl and massage it firmly with your fingers for 30 seconds to tenderize. Stir in the quinoa. Drizzle with half of the vinaigrette and toss to combine. Divide between 2 large shallow serving bowls. Top with the avocado and salmon fillets. Sprinkle with the pomegranate arils and drizzle with the remaining vinaigrette. Serve.

ORANGE SHRIMP AND BROCCOLI STIR-FRY

Makes 2 to 4 servings

Shrimp is one of my favorite proteins to use on busy weeknights when I haven't had the wherewithal to thaw meat or make it to the grocery store. I like to keep a bag of raw, frozen shrimp in the freezer. They thaw rapidly in a bowl of cold water and cook up in about 4 minutes flat, depending on the size of shrimp you buy.

1 pound raw large shrimp (21–30 per pound), peeled and deveined, tails left on

Salt and ground black pepper

2 tablespoons finely julienned orange peel

¼ cup freshly squeezed orange juice

½ cup + 2½ teaspoons water

2 tablespoons soy sauce

1 teaspoon rice wine vinegar

1 teaspoon Sriracha

2 tablespoons sugar

2½ teaspoons cornstarch

2 tablespoons canola oil, plus additional if needed

1 tablespoon sesame oil, plus additional if needed

6 cloves garlic, minced

1 tablespoon grated fresh ginger

1 pound broccoli, trimmed and cut into medium florets

2 teaspoons toasted sesame seeds

FOR SERVING:

Rice, steamed

Green onions, thinly sliced

Sriracha sauce or Chinese hot mustard

1 Pat the shrimp dry and season lightly with salt and pepper. Set aside. Set aside 1 tablespoon of the orange peel for serving.

2 In a small dish, stir together the remaining 1 tablespoon orange peel, orange juice, ½ cup of the water, soy sauce, vinegar, Sriracha, and sugar. In another small dish, stir together the cornstarch and 2½ teaspoons of the water. Set both aside.

3 Heat a wok or large nonstick skillet over medium-high heat. Add the canola oil and sesame oil. Cook the garlic and ginger for 1 minute, or until fragrant. Add the broccoli, season lightly with salt, and cook for 5 to 6 minutes, or until tender-crisp. Remove the broccoli from the pan and return the pan to the heat. Add more canola and sesame oil to the pan if needed, then add the shrimp in a single layer. Cook for 90 seconds, or until browned on the bottom, and then turn. Pour the orange mixture over the shrimp and bring to a boil. Return the broccoli to the pan. Stir in the cornstarch mixture and stir until the sauce has thickened. Sprinkle on the sesame seeds and toss well to coat.

4 To serve, sprinkle the reserved orange peel over top. Serve the hot stir-fry over steamed rice with the green onions and Sriracha sauce or Chinese hot mustard on the side.

POACHED HALIBUT
IN THAI COCONUT CURRY

Makes 4 servings

When I surveyed my readers on social media asking them which of my dishes needed to be included in the cookbook, this one was at the top of the list. One reader even won a cooking competition using this recipe! Giving the halibut fillets a quick gentle poach in this coconut curry broth prevents them from getting overcooked and dried out. I recommend serving this over steamed jasmine rice to soak up all of the lovely broth.

2 tablespoons olive oil, divided

1 large bunch greens, such as spinach, Swiss chard, or kale

Salt and ground black pepper

3 shallots, chopped

2 tablespoons Thai red curry paste

1 cup chicken broth

1 can (14 ounces) coconut milk

½ teaspoon sugar

4 fillets (4–6 ounces each) wild Alaska halibut

¼ cup cilantro, chopped

¼ cup sliced green onions (cut on the bias)

Juice of half a lime

FOR SERVING:

Cilantro, chopped

Green onions, sliced

2 cups steamed jasmine rice (optional)

½ lime, cut into wedges

1 In a deep skillet with a lid, heat 1 tablespoon of the olive oil over medium heat. Add the greens to the pan and season them generously with salt and pepper. Toss the greens in the oil until they just begin to wilt down and tenderize. Remove the greens to a bowl, cover to keep warm, and set aside. Wipe out the moisture from the pan and return to the heat.

2 Add the remaining 1 tablespoon olive oil to the pan. Cook the shallots, stirring frequently, for 2 minutes, or until tender and fragrant. Add the curry paste, chicken broth, coconut milk, and sugar. Bring to a simmer, reduce the heat to low, and cook for 10 minutes, or until the curry is reduced by half. Taste for seasoning and add salt, if needed.

recipe continues

3 Season the halibut fillets lightly with salt. Place them into the broth, spooning some of the broth over the top. Cover the pan and poach the fillets for 5 minutes (depending on the thickness of your fillets), or until cooked to medium-rare to medium, being very careful not to overcook (halibut dries out quickly, and we want to avoid that).

4 Distribute the sautéed greens evenly among 4 serving bowls. Carefully place a halibut fillet on top of each bed of greens.

5 To the curry broth, stir in the cilantro, green onions, and lime juice. Ladle some of the broth over each of the halibut fillets. Garnish with additional cilantro and green onions. Serve with steamed jasmine rice, if desired, and lime wedges.

GINGER PEANUT SALMON NOODLE BOWLS

Makes 6 servings

On one of our trips to Idaho to visit my wife's cousins, I was tasked with making dinner for a whole crew of their friends who were coming over. I knew immediately that I would make a version of these noodles, my go-to recipe for satisfying a hungry crowd. That night I used shrimp and chicken thighs as the proteins in the dish and added carrots to the mix of vegetables. Sometimes I use wide rice noodles, other times I use thin. This recipe is highly adaptable, so feel free to play around with the proteins and the vegetables in this one, customizing it to your liking. In this version, I'm using seared wild Alaska salmon fillets and crisp green snow peas. It's the addicting sauce and salty roasted peanuts on top that really make this recipe a tried-and-true crowd-pleaser.

FOR THE SAUCE:
⅓ cup soy sauce

¼ cup water

Juice of half a lime

¼ cup toasted sesame oil

3 tablespoons honey

3 tablespoons rice wine vinegar

4 cloves garlic

1 tablespoon chopped fresh ginger

3 tablespoons hoisin sauce

3 tablespoons peanut butter

6 fillets (4–6 ounces each) wild Alaska salmon, pin bones and skin removed

14 ounces rice noodles

1 tablespoon avocado or vegetable oil

1 large red bell pepper, julienned

1 cup snow peas

½ cup roasted salted peanuts, chopped

½ cup sliced green onions

½ cup cilantro, chopped

FOR SERVING:
1 lime, cut into wedges

Sriracha sauce

1 *To make the sauce:* In a blender, combine the soy sauce, water, lime juice, sesame oil, honey, vinegar, garlic, ginger, hoisin sauce, and peanut butter. Blend until smooth.

2 Place the salmon fillets in a resealable plastic bag and pour one-third of the sauce over the salmon to coat. (Reserve the remaining sauce.) Seal and marinate in the refrigerator for 30 minutes.

recipe continues

3 Meanwhile, begin preparing the rice noodles according to package directions.

4 In a large skillet, heat the oil over medium-high heat. Remove the salmon fillets from the marinade, shaking off the excess, and place them in the hot skillet. Sear for 3 minutes, or until browned on the bottom, and then turn and cook for 2 minutes for medium. Transfer the salmon to a plate and allow to rest. Add the bell pepper and snow peas to the skillet and cook, stirring constantly, for 2 to 3 minutes, or until heated through and tender-crisp. Add the reserved sauce to the skillet and heat through. Add the noodles to the pan and toss to coat with the sauce. Distribute the noodles and vegetables evenly among 6 serving bowls. Top each bowl with a salmon fillet. Sprinkle each plate generously with peanuts, green onions, and cilantro. Serve with lime wedges and Sriracha sauce on the side.

SCALLOP TOSTADAS WITH CORN SALSA AND CHIPOTLE CREMA

Makes 4

Scallops are quite possibly my favorite seafood. If I go to a restaurant and there's a scallop special on offer, I can't help but order it. They're plump and mild, slightly sweet, with just a hint of the briny sea. They're fun to work with in the kitchen, too. They cook very quickly and take well to many different flavors and preparations.

The trick to getting a good sear on the outside of the scallop is to pat them dry before cooking them in a very hot pan. Don't cook them too long; otherwise, they go from delightfully tender to annoyingly chewy. Scallops are also outstanding served raw and thinly sliced in a citrusy crudo. For raw preparations especially, be sure to ask for "dry" scallops, which are the freshest option with the purest scallop flavor.

1 tablespoon avocado oil

4 corn tortillas

Salt

FOR THE CORN SALSA:

1 cup corn

¼ cup finely chopped poblano chile pepper

¼ cup finely chopped red bell pepper

¼ cup finely chopped red onion

¼ cup cilantro, finely chopped

Juice of half a lime

¼ teaspoon sugar

Salt

FOR THE CHIPOTLE CREMA:

¼ cup sour cream

2 tablespoons milk

1 tablespoon adobo sauce from a can of chipotles in adobo

1 tablespoon lime juice

½ teaspoon garlic powder

Salt

FOR THE SCALLOPS:

2 tablespoons avocado oil

2 tablespoons adobo sauce from a can of chipotles in adobo

12 large Alaska scallops, patted dry

Salt

FOR SERVING:

1 avocado, pitted, peeled, and sliced

1 lime, cut into wedges

1 In a small skillet, heat the avocado oil over medium heat. Fry the corn tortillas on both sides until golden brown and crisp. Transfer the tortillas to a plated lined with paper towels to drain. Season with salt to taste and keep warm.

2 *To make the corn salsa:* In a bowl, stir together the corn, poblano pepper, bell pepper, onion, cilantro, lime juice, and sugar. Season with salt to taste. Cover and refrigerate until ready to assemble tostadas.

recipe continues

3 *To make the chipotle crema:* In a small bowl, whisk together the sour cream, milk, adobo sauce, lime juice, and garlic powder until smooth. Season generously with salt. Cover and refrigerate until ready to serve.

4 *To make the scallops:* In a large cast-iron skillet, heat the avocado oil over medium-high heat. Stir the adobo sauce into the oil. Season the scallops with salt to taste and add them to the hot pan. Sear the scallops for 3 minutes, or until browned and caramel-ized on the bottom. Turn and sear on the other side, 2 to 3 minutes (depending on the size of your scallops). Be careful not to overcook the scallops. Transfer the scallops to a plate.

5 To assemble the tostadas, Top each crisp tortilla with a heaping spoonful of corn salsa. Place 3 seared scallops on top of each tostada, followed by avocado slices. Drizzle with chipotle crema. Serve promptly with lime wedges on the side.

KING CRAB PASTA WITH HOMEMADE SOURDOUGH BREAD CRUMBS

Makes 4 servings

My oldest son Brady's two most requested foods are sushi and crab. I can't imagine where he inherited such a sophisticated and [cough cough] expensive palate. Wink. When I asked him what he wanted for Christmas, he dryly declared, "Crab." Although I couldn't afford to serve a king crab leg dinner to feed 6 on Christmas Day, I made a buttery king crab pasta, which was fancy enough for the holiday occasion but didn't break the bank.

Alaskans love sourdough, a throwback to the Alaska Gold Rush, when our miners were called Sourdoughs. Some Alaskans maintain sourdough starters that go back generations, keeping them on hand for loaves of bread and stacks of pancakes. Sourdough also makes terrific homemade bread crumbs, which add some welcome texture and rich nuttiness to this crab pasta, soaking up all the delicious sauce in the process.

FOR THE SOURDOUGH BREAD CRUMBS:

4 ounces day-old sourdough bread, sliced

1 tablespoon butter

1 tablespoon extra-virgin olive oil

½ teaspoon kosher salt

1 clove garlic, minced

1 tablespoon chopped parsley

Zest of 1 lemon

FOR THE PASTA:

1 pound spaghetti rigati

4 tablespoons butter

1 tablespoon extra-virgin olive oil

2 cloves garlic, minced

¼ teaspoon red-pepper flakes

½ cup dry white wine or Prosecco

2 tablespoons lemon juice

1 teaspoon lemon zest

1 pound lump Alaska king crab meat

½ cup freshly grated Parmesan cheese

Salt

FOR SERVING:

Parmesan cheese, shaved

Parsley, finely chopped

Red-pepper flakes

1 *To make the sourdough bread crumbs:* Preheat the oven to 300°F. Lay the bread slices on a large sheet pan. Bake for 15 to 20 minutes, or until dried out. Allow the bread to cool. Place in a food processor and process into crumbs.

2 In a skillet, heat the butter and olive oil over medium heat. Stir in 1½ cups of sourdough bread crumbs. Cook, stirring often, until the bread crumbs begin to toast and smell fragrant. Add the salt, garlic, parsley, and lemon zest, stirring well to combine. Remove from the heat and allow the bread crumbs to cool while you make the pasta.

3 *To make the pasta:* Prepare the spaghetti according to package directions.

4 In a large skillet, heat the butter and olive oil over medium heat. Add the garlic and red-pepper flakes and cook for 90 seconds, or until fragrant. Pour the wine into the pan and allow to simmer and reduce for 5 minutes. Remove from the heat. Add the lemon juice and zest, crab meat, spaghetti, and cheese, tossing briefly to coat. Season with salt to taste. Sprinkle the sourdough bread crumbs over top of the pasta. Serve in pasta bowls with shaved Parmesan, chopped parsley, and additional red-pepper flakes as desired.

SMOKED SALMON POT PIE
WITH CHIVE DROP BISCUITS

Makes 4 to 6 servings

Pot pies are a wintertime staple at our house and in many homes in Alaska.
One of my favorite ways to make a pot pie is in a cast-iron skillet with
fluffy buttermilk drop biscuits on top. Drop biscuits are less labor intensive
than a traditional 2-crust pot pie, and they require much less baking time, too.
But don't think that less work means it'll be any less satisfying and delicious.
The rich smoked salmon filling is brightened by fresh dill and lemon
zest, all topped with buttery biscuits freckled with green chives.

FOR THE FILLING:
2 tablespoons butter

1 onion, finely chopped

1/4 cup all-purpose flour

2 cups chicken broth

1 cup milk

1 1/2 cups canned smoked
salmon, drained and flaked

1 1/2 cups frozen peas
and carrots

1 tablespoon fresh dill,
finely chopped

1 teaspoon lemon zest

Freshly cracked black pepper

*FOR THE CHIVE DROP
BISCUITS:*
2 cups all-purpose flour

1 tablespoon baking powder

1/4 teaspoon baking soda

1/2 teaspoon salt

2 teaspoons sugar

2 tablespoons finely chopped
fresh chives

6 tablespoons cold butter

1 1/4 cups buttermilk

Freshly cracked black pepper

Old Bay seasoning

1 *To make the filling:* In a 12" cast-iron skillet, melt the butter over medium heat. Cook the onion, stirring frequently, for 3 minutes, or until translucent. Sprinkle in the flour and cook, stirring constantly, for 1 to 2 minutes (this helps eliminate a "floury" taste in your filling, so don't skip this step).

2 Pour in the chicken broth and milk and stir until combined. Increase the heat to medium high and bring the

mixture to a gentle boil. Reduce the heat to low and simmer for 10 minutes, stirring occasionally as the mixture thickens. Add the smoked salmon, peas and carrots, dill, and lemon zest. Season to taste with cracked black pepper.

NOTE: Smoked salmon is often quite salty on its own, so do not add salt to the filling until after adding the smoked salmon and checking the salt level. The filling may not need any salt.

3 Preheat the oven to 425°F.

4 *To make the chive drop biscuits:* Meanwhile, in a mixing bowl, stir together the flour, baking powder, baking soda, salt, sugar, and chives. Using a pastry blender, cut in the butter until the mixture is crumbly. Add the buttermilk, stirring until the mixture just comes together and forms a thick, sticky dough (be careful not to overwork the dough; this is the key to a fluffy biscuit).

5 To assemble the pot pie, drop the biscuit dough in ¼-cup dollops onto the top of the pot pie filling. Sprinkle the biscuits with black pepper and Old Bay seasoning to taste. Bake for 18 to 20 minutes, or until the biscuits are golden and the filling is bubbly. Serve promptly.

HONEY SRIRACHA SEARED SCALLOPS OVER MISO QUINOA

Makes 2 servings

Not only do I enjoy scallops for their remarkable flavor and quick cooking time, but they are also a healthy and sustainable seafood option. This yummy miso-dressed quinoa bowl topped with sticky honey Sriracha scallops is impressive enough to serve to a special guest, but quick enough to make on a busy weeknight. It's always good to have a few entrée recipes like this in your arsenal that are versatile enough for most any evening.

FOR THE MISO QUINOA:

1 cup uncooked quinoa

2 cups chicken broth

2 teaspoons miso paste

1 tablespoon rice wine vinegar

2 teaspoons lime juice

1 tablespoon dark sesame oil

1 tablespoon peanut oil

1 teaspoon grated fresh ginger

1 clove garlic, minced

¼ cup chopped cilantro

¼ cup sliced green onions

FOR THE SCALLOPS:

4 tablespoons butter

2 cloves garlic, minced

1 tablespoon Sriracha

1 tablespoon honey

10 large Alaska scallops, patted dry

Salt

1 *To make the miso quinoa:* Rinse the quinoa well in a fine-mesh sieve under cold water. Transfer the rinsed quinoa to a saucepan and add the chicken broth. Cover and bring to a boil over high heat. Reduce the heat to low and simmer for 12 minutes, or until the quinoa is tender and the liquid is absorbed. Fluff with a fork, remove from the heat, and keep covered until ready to serve.

2 Meanwhile, in a small bowl, whisk together the miso paste, vinegar, lime juice, sesame and peanut oils, ginger, and garlic until combined. When the quinoa is ready, stir in the cilantro, green onions, and miso dressing. Set aside.

3 *To make the scallops:* In a cast-iron skillet, melt the butter over medium-high heat. Add the garlic, Sriracha, and honey and cook, stirring constantly, until bubbling and fragrant. Season the scallops with salt to taste and add them to the hot pan. Sear the scallops for 3 minutes, or until browned and caramelized on the bottoms. Turn and sear on the other side for 2 to 3 minutes (depending on the size of your scallops), being careful not to overcook. Promptly remove the scallops from the heat and transfer them to a plate.

4 To plate the dish, evenly distribute the miso quinoa between 2 serving bowls. Top each bowl of quinoa with 5 seared scallops. Drizzle any remaining pan juices from the Sriracha honey mixture over the scallops. Serve promptly.

4 / ALASKA EVENINGS
MAIN DISHES

MAIN DISHES

RICOTTA GNOCCHI IN SPICY TOMATO
SAUCE WITH BASIL AND FRESH
MOZZARELLA *110*

KENAI CHEESEBURGERS *114*

KENAI CHEESE DIP *116*

CHICKPEA AND MANGO CURRY
WITH SPINACH *117*

HOMEMADE FLATBREAD *119*

BISON AND SMOKED PORTER PIE WITH
MUSHROOMS *122*

GRILLED TERIYAKI CHICKEN SALAD
WITH SESAME DRESSING *125*

BAKED CHICKEN WINGS WITH
BOURBON BIRCH SYRUP GLAZE *127*

FLATIRON STEAK WITH ASPARAGUS
AND BLUE CHEESE *130*

CHRIS TRUE'S MARINADE *133*

CAST-IRON BARBECUE CHICKEN
PIZZAS *135*

HUNTER'S PIE *137*

JALAPEÑO POPPER MACARONI
AND CHEESE *140*

CHIPOTLE CHICKEN ENCHILADAS
WITH ROASTED BUTTERNUT SQUASH
AND BLACK BEANS *143*

ALASKA HOT DOGS WITH HARD CIDER
CARAMELIZED ONIONS *147*

SHEET PAN BALSAMIC CHICKEN
WITH BRUSSELS SPROUTS
AND SWEET POTATOES *148*

*M*aking food and being in the kitchen is like therapy for me. I can step into my safe space for a moment, get into the zone, and cook my heart out. It's not about eating; it's about the process of it all. It is in the kitchen where I feel centered and focused, creative and self-aware. It's my way of practicing mindfulness. Just me and those ingredients and the recipes writing themselves in my head. In all of the hardest moments of my life, cooking has always helped me find my way back home.

In *The Rainbow Comes and Goes,* Anderson Cooper writes to his mother, Gloria Vanderbilt, these words: "I've often thought of loss as a kind of language. Once learned, it's never forgotten. . . . It would be easier, in a way, if people knew without my having to say anything that I am not whole, that part of me died long ago." Yes, Anderson. So much yes.

Some losses are huge and sudden. The kind that shock you and take your breath away, happening in a moment and leaving you never the same. Then there are other losses that are slow and pervasive, happening gradually over time, an inescapable grief. It's hard to know who you might have been without the loss because it has seemingly always been there.

When my mother graduated from high school, she took a graduation trip to Hawaii and ended up not returning home, staying there on the islands for 8 years. It was there that she met my father and made a life with him. I know very little about this time in my mother's life. I was only a toddler when she left my father and returned to the mainland from Hawaii. After that, she hardly ever spoke of him. She didn't keep any photos of my father, and I didn't know his name until later in adulthood. Although I was much too young to remember the moment my father and I were separated, it has stayed with me my entire life, like an unshakable void, or a language never forgotten, as Anderson puts it, shaping me in ways even I can't fully understand. It markedly shaped my mother, too, and the complex unspoken dynamic between us. There are questions that would never be answered, words that would never be uttered, and ultimately two women, mother and daughter, who would never quite understand each other. I can safely say that I understand her better now than I ever did when she was living.

It was after I moved to Alaska and during my first year as a food blogger when my mother was diagnosed with Stage IV pancreatic cancer at the age of 57. I flew to Hawaii (where she had returned after I went to college) and stayed for 3 weeks providing her home hospice care. Her death was slow and painful, but I count it a tremendous privilege to have been there, and I wouldn't trade those profound, agonizing moments for anything in the world.

When I returned to my life in Alaska, to my three young children, to my food blog, I was changed. Or rather, I was in the process of being changed by this new loss. I took my grief with me into the kitchen and allowed it to anchor there, making that the place where I could permit myself to feel it, to try to come to terms with it. Gradually, things within me began to shift and give way, like a glacier when it calves into the sea. *Crack. Shudder. Rumble. Splash.* So much of who I had become was in response to, or reaction against, who my mother was. Now that she was gone, those things no longer had anywhere to land in me.

As long as I could remember, I had been a die-hard people pleaser. This was a result of who my mother was. I wanted nothing more than her attention and affection, for her to be consistently present with me, so I tried to earn it. As I grew, my people-pleasing permeated my entire life—my relationships, my parenting, my food blog, my identity. I prided myself on being pleasant, accommodating, and quiet.

> GRADUALLY, THINGS WITHIN ME BEGAN TO SHIFT AND GIVE WAY, LIKE A GLACIER WHEN IT CALVES INTO THE SEA. *CRACK. SHUDDER. RUMBLE. SPLASH.*

Sometimes invisible and voiceless, always aware of everyone around me, but with no idea what Maya wanted or needed. I often had no opinion, or rather was so out of touch with my opinion after years of stifling it that I couldn't access it at all. I believed the lie that making myself small made people happy. I believed that I made people's lives easier by getting out of the way. I believed that people would love me or be there for me only if I was who they expected me to be. I was still that same hungry little girl on the playground, on the outside of my life looking in. I did everything for others, neglecting myself, and it left me feeling deeply lonely, deeply unseen, and deeply unheard. My mother was gone. It was time to try to move on from this way of being that had so defined me.

Little by little, I began to get in touch with myself and to gain confidence in my own voice. It was first evident in my blogging. Where once I felt unworthy of being a food blogger, convinced of all the ways I wasn't good enough, I began to lean in it with purpose and resolve. My photography grew, and my style started to take shape and solidify, becoming more a reflection of me. I was willing to take bigger risks in the kitchen, suddenly beginning to believe in myself at last.

One of the formerly unthinkable risks I was willing to take was to attempt to make gnocchi from scratch like Mario Batali. Mario was my first chef crush when I was in high school; the depth of his knowledge about food and its origins is staggering, and the effortless way he moves about the kitchen is captivating. I couldn't get enough of his show *Molto Mario,* complete with his trademark orange clogs and the Italian operatic ditty that played before and after every commercial break. It was Mario who long ago taught me the value of good extra-virgin olive oil and how to salt pasta water like the sea. He taught me that Parmigiano-Reggiano has absolutely nothing to do with powder in a green can, and that one of the most important phrases in the kitchen is *al dente.* Fast-forward about 15 years, and that high schooler is now a food blogger, standing in her kitchen, mourning the loss of her mother, attempting to make gnocchi for the first time in her life, all because of Mario Batali and the fine culinary education one can get from watching food television. I had never traveled the world or been to Italy. I can't speak Italian, and I can't pronounce all the food terminology properly the way Mario does (although I try). I have never been to culinary school. But, gosh darn it, I was gonna make gnocchi anyway.

Gnocchi became my therapy. I made it several times in the months after my mother's death, trying different recipes and techniques, learning as I went. I lost myself in the process of it—getting flour all over my hands, working the tender dough, rolling it into long snakes, cutting the pasta with a bench scraper, and finally, the best part, pressing fine grooves into each nugget of pasta by running it down the length of the wooden gnocchi board. When I would put a pot of water to boil on the stove in winter, all of the windows in the house would get covered with a steamy layer of fog, obscuring my view. Condensation began to build up and drip down the glass, like the tears of grief I couldn't shed.

After a quick dip in the tumultuous water, salty like the sea, the gnocchi floated to the top and needed to be immediately fished out and transferred to the spicy tomato sauce I had waiting. I scattered plump, creamy balls of mozzarella fresca atop the simmering sauce just before serving, so that it just began to melt and form strings when it was time to plate. Finally, I cut the fresh basil into a chiffonade and sprinkled it generously on top like crinkly paper confetti. When it was all done, I wanted to curl up in those cozy pillows of gnocchi and take a long nap, the way I feel after a good, deep therapy session. It's one of my all-time favorite meals to cook and to eat, for both the phenomenal flavors and the bittersweet memories. My Italian wife and my oldest son both love it, too, and request it often. That loss, and the gnocchi therapy that followed, were just the beginning of a new chapter taking shape in my life. And I can't be anything but thankful as I take a seat at the table and take it all in with each bite.

RICOTTA GNOCCHI IN SPICY TOMATO SAUCE WITH BASIL AND FRESH MOZZARELLA

Makes 4 servings

Ricotta gnocchi is less labor intensive than traditional potato gnocchi, which makes it a great option for gnocchi novices and busy families. But don't feel like you'd be getting a lesser product. The ricotta yields a rich, tender dumpling and adds a fair amount more protein to your pasta than any potato would. I like to keep the sauce extremely simple with olive oil, garlic, and a fair amount of red-pepper flakes, which highlights the pure flavors of the fresh mozzarella and the delicate gnocchi. A generous handful of fresh basil is the perfect finishing touch.

FOR THE RICOTTA GNOCCHI:

1 pound whole milk ricotta cheese

1 egg, lightly beaten

1½ cups all-purpose flour, plus additional as needed

¼ teaspoon salt

FOR THE SPICY TOMATO SAUCE:

1 tablespoon extra-virgin olive oil

3 cloves garlic, minced

½ teaspoon crushed red-pepper flakes

1 can (15 ounces) plain tomato sauce

1 teaspoon sugar

Salt

8 ounces fresh mozzarella, cut into bite-size cubes

¼ cup fresh basil, cut into a chiffonade

1 *To make the ricotta gnocchi:* In a mixing bowl, stir together the ricotta and egg until smooth. Add the flour and salt, folding gently into the ricotta to combine. If the dough is sticky, add more flour by the tablespoon until the dough is workable and no longer sticky, but still quite soft. *Do not knead or overmix the dough, as this will result in dense, chewy gnocchi.*

2 Turn the dough out onto a floured surface and pinch off baseball-size portions of dough. Using both hands in a back-and-forth motion, roll each ball of dough into a long snake, about ½" to ¾" thick. (The size of the dumplings doesn't matter as much as that they are uniform with one another so they cook evenly.) Using a bench cutter or knife, cut the snake into 1" pieces. Press each gnocchi down a wooden gnocchi board or the tines of a fork to make groove marks. The grooves help hold the sauce.

3 Place a large pot of water over high heat. Salt generously and bring to a boil.

4 *To make the spicy tomato sauce:* While the water comes to a boil, in a large skillet, heat the olive oil over medium heat. Cook the garlic and red-pepper flakes, stirring, for 1 minute, or until fragrant but without browning the garlic. Add the tomato sauce to the pan, followed by the sugar. Stir to combine. Season with salt to taste. Reduce the heat to medium low and simmer while the gnocchi are cooking.

5 When the water is boiling steadily, carefully drop the gnocchi in. Grab a large slotted spoon. As soon as the gnocchi float to the top, they are done. *If you overcook them, they will turn into mush, so remove them promptly.* As you gradually remove the gnocchi, shake off the excess water and put them into the pan of sauce, stirring to coat. When all of the gnocchi have been transferred to the sauce, remove the pan from the heat. Toss in the mozzarella and basil. Fold gently to combine. The mozzarella will begin to melt, so don't stir much. Serve immediately.

KENAI CHEESEBURGERS

Makes 4

One recipe this part of Alaska is known for is its world-famous Kenai cheese dip. They make a mild and a spicy version; I tend to opt for the spicier version, which includes red-pepper flakes. The addicting combination of Cheddar cheese, jalapeños, garlic, and liquid smoke makes for a tasty spread on crackers or a dip for corn chips. But when placed atop a sizzling burger patty and fired under the broiler until melted and bubbly, it makes an outstanding cheeseburger. If you're not familiar with liquid smoke, it can typically be found in a small bottle near the barbecue sauces at your local market.

4 ground beef hamburger patties (¼–⅓ pound each)

Salt and ground black pepper

2 tablespoons avocado oil

½ cup Kenai Cheese Dip (page 116)

FOR SERVING:

4 hamburger buns, toasted

4 thick slices tomato

4 slices red onion

4 crisp lettuce leaves

4 tablespoons barbecue sauce

1 Preheat the broiler to high.

2 Season the hamburger patties liberally with salt and pepper on both sides. In a cast-iron skillet, heat the avocado oil over medium-high heat. Sear the hamburgers, covering the pan to prevent oil splatter, for 3 minutes, or until browned on the bottoms. Turn and sear on the other side for 2 to 3 minutes. Place about 2 tablespoons of Kenai Cheese Dip on top of each patty, flattening it down a bit. Turn off the heat and transfer the skillet to the oven. Broil the burgers for 2 minutes, or until the cheese begins to bubble and melt and a thermometer inserted in the center registers 160°F.

3 To assemble the burgers, place a cheeseburger patty onto each bottom bun. Top with the tomato, onion, and lettuce. Smear 1 tablespoon of barbecue sauce onto the inside of each top bun. Cover the burgers with the top buns and serve.

KENAI CHEESE DIP

Makes about 2 cups

½ cup mayonnaise

¼ cup canned or jarred jalapeño chile peppers, chopped

2 tablespoons jalapeño juice (from the can or jar)

½ teaspoon garlic powder

½ teaspoon smoked paprika

½ teaspoon red-pepper flakes

¼ teaspoon liquid smoke

Pinch of salt

1½ cups grated Cheddar cheese

In a mixing bowl, stir together the mayonnaise, jalapeño peppers, jalapeño juice, garlic powder, smoked paprika, red-pepper flakes, liquid smoke, and salt. Fold in the cheese until well combined. Store covered in the refrigerator until ready to use. Use on top of Kenai Cheeseburgers or as a cold dip for corn chips and crackers.

CHICKPEA AND MANGO CURRY WITH SPINACH

Makes 3 to 4 servings

My favorite proteins to serve in homemade Indian curries are chicken, lentils, and chickpeas. But where chicken and lentils have a longer cooking time, chickpeas are fast. Keep a couple of cans of chickpeas (typically labeled garbanzo beans) in your pantry, along with some coconut milk, and you'll be well on your way to a quick and easy meatless dinner. This is great served over steamed rice, but our favorite way to enjoy it is with this homemade flatbread.

1 tablespoon vegetable oil

1 tablespoon curry powder

1 teaspoon garam masala

Pinch of cayenne pepper (or to taste)

½ teaspoon salt

1 onion, chopped

2 cloves garlic, minced

1 teaspoon finely chopped fresh ginger

1 can (13.5 ounces) coconut milk

½ cup plain tomato sauce

1 can (15 ounces) chickpeas, rinsed and drained

1 cup chopped mango

3 ounces baby spinach leaves

2 teaspoons lemon juice

In a Dutch oven, heat the oil over medium heat. Add the curry powder, garam masala, and cayenne pepper. Toast the spices, stirring often, for 2 minutes. Stir in the salt. Add the onion, garlic, and ginger and cook, stirring frequently, for 2 minutes, or until the onion is tender. Pour in the coconut milk, tomato sauce, and chickpeas. Cook, stirring often, for 5 minutes, or until heated through. Turn off the heat and stir in the mango and spinach, folding the spinach in until it just begins to wilt. Add the lemon juice and season with additional salt as needed to taste. Serve promptly with flatbread.

HOMEMADE FLATBREAD

Makes 4 servings

½ cup butter, softened until it can be stirred

2 cups all-purpose flour

½ teaspoon salt

¼ teaspoon baking powder

⅔ cup hot water (about 110°F)

1 In a mixing bowl, combine the butter, flour, salt, and baking powder. Stir until the mixture is combined and somewhat crumbly. Gradually add the hot water, stirring until a ball of dough forms. (You may not need to use all of the water.) Allow the dough to rest for 20 minutes. Break the dough off into wads the size of a golf ball. Using a rolling pin, roll the dough out on a floured surface until quite thin. Repeat with the remaining dough.

2 Place a large nonstick skillet over medium-high heat. Coat the pan lightly with vegetable oil. Place 1 flatbread into the pan and cook for 90 seconds, or until it begins to bubble and brown on the bottom. Turn and cook for 60 to 90 seconds, or until brown on the other side. Keep warm while cooking the remaining dough, adding more oil as needed between flatbreads. Serve the flatbread warm with Chickpea and Mango Curry with Spinach.

BISON AND SMOKED PORTER PIE
WITH MUSHROOMS

Makes 4 to 6 servings

Bison, both massive and majestic, are often overlooked as one of Alaska's great game meats. Bison has a mild flavor, is quite tender, and is leaner than beef. It works well in stews, braises, and a steak and ale pie like this one. Bison is becoming more popular, and therefore more widely available, but if you can't find any near you, 2 pounds of cubed chuck beef roast is a great substitute. As for the beer, I used a robust smoked porter from Alaskan Brewing Company, but any good dark beer should work nicely.

2 tablespoons vegetable oil

¼ cup all-purpose flour

2 pounds bison, cubed

4 slices bacon, chopped

1 medium yellow onion, chopped

1 clove garlic, minced

1½ cups smoked porter, divided

3 tablespoons Worcestershire sauce

2 tablespoons tomato paste

2 teaspoons sugar

1 tablespoon flat-leaf parsley leaves, chopped

2 teaspoons fresh thyme, chopped

1 cup beef broth

3 ounces mushrooms, quartered

Salt and ground black pepper

1 tablespoon cornstarch

1 tablespoon cold water

1 sheet puff pastry

1 egg, beaten

1 Preheat the oven to 300°F.

2 In a 12" cast-iron skillet, heat the oil over medium-high heat. Place the flour in a resealable plastic bag. Add the bison, seal, and shake to coat. Sear the bison until browned on all sides. Transfer to a plate and set aside. Add the bacon to the pan and cook until browned and crisp. Reduce the heat to medium and add the onion and garlic. Cook until the onion is tender and fragrant.

3 Deglaze the pan with ¾ cup of the porter, scraping the bottom of the pan. Simmer for 2 minutes. Add the Worcestershire sauce, tomato paste, sugar, parsley, and thyme, stirring until well combined. Add the remaining ¾ cup smoked porter and the beef broth. Stir in the mushrooms and seared bison. Season with salt and pepper to taste. Carefully cover the skillet with foil and bake for 2 hours. Remove the foil and bake uncovered for 30 minutes.

4 Remove the skillet from the oven. Increase the heat to 400°F. In a small bowl, mix the cornstarch and cold water together until smooth. Stir into the filling mixture to thicken. Place the puff pastry sheet over the top of the filling.

Cut a few slices in the center to vent. Using a pastry brush, brush the puff pastry with the beaten egg. Bake for 30 minutes, or until the puff pastry is golden and cooked through. Serve in bowls.

GRILLED TERIYAKI CHICKEN SALAD WITH SESAME DRESSING

Makes 4 servings

When my mother was still alive and living on the Big Island of Hawaii, I would make occasional trips to visit her and my younger brother. As soon as I would step off the plane, the humidity and the heat were formidable, particularly when one is accustomed to the climate in Alaska. While there, I would often help cook. I would crave crisp green salads, fresh fruit and vegetables, and any excuse not to turn on the oven. Once I made a version of this chicken salad with a bright, acidic sesame dressing. After that, my brother requested I make this salad every time I returned to Hawaii. The vibrant rainbow of colors in this salad reminds me distinctly of my mother and the bright color palette she used when painting tropical Hawaiian flowers and birds.

This recipe is highly adaptable and forgiving. Use what you have that is seasonal and available. In place of snow peas, try snap peas or edamame. Napa cabbage would be splendid in exchange for the red cabbage. For added crunch, toss in some crispy fried wonton strips as well. To finish, I add a few drops of fiery hot sesame oil to my own plate. I love the bright red color of the oil and the way the heat sneaks up on you.

recipe continues

FOR THE TERIYAKI CHICKEN:

½ cup soy sauce

½ cup brown sugar

1 teaspoon grated fresh ginger

1 pound boneless, skinless chicken breasts

2 teaspoons sesame seeds

FOR THE SESAME DRESSING:

½ cup rice wine vinegar

¼ cup sesame oil

2 teaspoons Sriracha

1 teaspoon soy sauce

1 teaspoon granulated sugar

FOR THE SALAD:

16 ounces mixed greens

1 cup finely shredded red cabbage

1 red bell pepper, julienned

1 cup fresh snow peas

1 large carrot, shaved into ribbons

⅓ cup sliced green onions

⅓ cup cilantro, chopped

⅓ cup sliced almonds, toasted

1 tablespoon sesame seeds

FOR SERVING:

Hot sesame oil

1 *To make the teriyaki chicken:* In a shallow dish, whisk together the soy sauce, brown sugar, and ginger until the sugar is dissolved. Submerge the chicken in the marinade. Cover and refrigerate for 30 minutes. Preheat the grill to medium high. Grill for 10 minutes, turning once, or until a thermometer inserted in the thickest portion registers 165°F and the juices run clear. Remove from the heat to rest for 5 minutes. Sprinkle the chicken with the sesame seeds and slice on the bias.

2 *To make the sesame dressing:* In a small bowl, whisk together the vinegar, sesame oil, Sriracha, soy sauce, and granulated sugar until well combined. Set aside until ready to serve.

3 *To assemble the salad:* Place the greens in a large bowl. Add most of the cabbage, bell pepper, snow peas, carrot, green onions, cilantro, almonds, and sesame seeds, reserving some for the top of the salad. Drizzle on half of the sesame dressing and toss the salad well to coat and combine. Top with the remaining toppings and the sliced chicken. Drizzle the remaining dressing over top. Serve promptly with hot sesame oil on the side.

BAKED CHICKEN WINGS
WITH BOURBON BIRCH SYRUP GLAZE

Makes 4 servings

I wasn't a wing eater until my wife came along. She introduced me to her passion for the game of hockey by taking me to the local sports bar in Soldotna to watch the Boston Bruins over a finger-licking plate of buffalo wings. She taught this timid girl that it's okay to hoot and holler at the television screen in public, especially while your hands and face are slathered with sauce. Her boldness is contagious, her enthusiasm catching. Now, when I go to the local rink to watch her and her team play hockey, I hoot and holler like the best of them. She is my favorite hockey player, and I've come to love the game. And I also make chicken wings at home now, experimenting with different sauce recipes, because I've come to love wings, too.

Birch syrup is a unique Alaska ingredient, not as sweet as maple syrup, and not unlike sorghum. There's a distinct woodiness to it, perhaps a bit of neighboring spruce from the boreal forest. If you don't have birch syrup, pure maple syrup can be substituted with great results.

2 pounds chicken wings

Salt and ground black pepper

4 tablespoons butter

2 tablespoons finely chopped onion

2 cloves garlic, minced

½ cup bourbon

⅓ cup birch syrup or pure maple syrup

1 tablespoon Sriracha

1 Preheat the oven to 425°F. Line a large rimmed baking sheet with foil. Place a metal rack on top of the baking sheet. This will allow the chicken to get crispy on both sides and allow the juices to run off onto the foil. Place the chicken wings in a single layer on top of the rack. Season generously with salt and pepper. Bake for 30 minutes.

2 Meanwhile, in a saucepan, melt the butter over medium heat. When the butter is bubbling, add the onion and garlic and cook for 1 minute. Pour in the bourbon, birch or maple syrup, and Sriracha. Reduce the heat and simmer for 3 to 5 minutes, or until thick and sticky. Keep warm.

recipe continues

3 Remove the pan of wings from the oven. Turn the broiler to high. Using tongs, transfer the wings to a heatproof mixing bowl. Pour two-thirds of the sauce over the wings and, using the tongs or a wooden spoon, toss the wings to coat. Return the wings to the metal rack. Broil for 6 to 10 minutes, turning once, or until caramelized on both sides. Drizzle the remaining sauce over the wings just prior to serving.

FLATIRON STEAK WITH ASPARAGUS AND BLUE CHEESE

Makes 2 to 4 servings

I'm the first to admit that steaks have not typically been my strong suit. It's not that I don't enjoy them or can't cook them; I just don't feel quite as confident preparing them as I do with most other things in the kitchen. And when we moved to Alaska, I nearly gave up making red meat altogether because it's pretty darn expensive here, since Alaska is not exactly livestock country. Instead I opted for proteins that were more affordable to feed my family.

Acknowledging my lack of confidence with steak, I turned to our friend and neighbor, Chris True, who is a pro in the meat and grilling department. Chris makes one badass steak, so I asked him to share his secrets with me. He recommended flatiron steak—an extremely inexpensive cut of meat, but oh so tender, with lots of fine marbling throughout. It cooks quickly, and 1 steak sliced on the bias can serve several people. I was sold. Why had no one told me this before? Chris also shared with me his go-to marinade recipe for red meat and game, which he was so kind to jot down for the cookbook, since he's more of a cooking on the fly kind of guy.

So I went to the local butcher shop and purchased my first-ever flatiron steak. I brought it home, tenderized it, and soaked it in Chris True's steak marinade overnight. Then I broiled it for 4 minutes per side for medium-rare to medium, in the same pan as the asparagus and lemon. After a 10-minute rest, I sliced the steak and sprinkled it with blue cheese. It's the best damn steak I've ever made, hands down. And it was so quick and easy; with just 8 minutes of broiling time and a 10-minute rest, dinner can be on the table in 20 minutes flat. All thanks to Chris.

P.S. This recipe would be stellar with mashed red potatoes on the side to soak up all the yummy juices.

recipe continues

1¾ pounds flatiron steak

1 recipe Chris True's Marinade (page 133)

1 bunch asparagus, trimmed

1 tablespoon extra-virgin olive oil

Sea salt and freshly cracked black pepper

1 lemon, sliced in half

2 ounces blue cheese, crumbled

1 Using a meat tenderizer, tenderize the steak on both sides. Place in a resealable plastic bag and cover with the marinade. Seal and refrigerate for at least 8 hours, or up to 24.

2 Place the oven rack in the top position and preheat the broiler to high. Line a large rimmed baking sheet with foil. Place the asparagus on the baking sheet. Drizzle with the olive oil and toss the asparagus to coat. Season with the salt and pepper to taste. Position the asparagus in a single layer around the outside of the pan, leaving room for the steak in the center.

3 Remove the steak from the marinade and shake off any excess marinade. Place the steak on the middle of the baking sheet. Place the lemon slices cut side down on the baking sheet in opposite corners.

4 Broil the steak and asparagus for 4 minutes. Remove the pan from the oven and turn the steak. Broil for 4 minutes on the other side for medium-rare to medium. Allow the steak to rest for 10 minutes.

5 Transfer the steak to a cutting board and slice it on the bias. Return the steak slices to the pan and sprinkle them with the blue cheese. Serve the steak promptly with the broiled asparagus, finishing with squeezes of the lemon halves and a drizzle of the pan juices over top of everything.

CHRIS TRUE'S MARINADE

Makes enough for up to 4 pounds of steak or wild game

$\frac{1}{2}$ cup soy sauce

$\frac{1}{4}$ cup apple cider vinegar

2 tablespoons
Worcestershire sauce

1 tablespoon lemon juice

1 tablespoon brown sugar

1 tablespoon chili powder

2 teaspoons ground cumin

1 teaspoon garlic powder

$\frac{1}{4}$ teaspoon cayenne pepper

$\frac{1}{2}$ teaspoon freshly cracked
black pepper

$\frac{1}{4}$ teaspoon sea salt

In a bowl, stir together the soy sauce, vinegar, Worcestershire sauce, lemon juice, brown sugar, chili powder, cumin, garlic powder, cayenne pepper, black pepper, and salt until well combined and the sugar has dissolved. Use to marinate steaks or wild game for grilling or broiling, like Flatiron Steak with Asparagus and Blue Cheese (page 130).

CAST-IRON BARBECUE CHICKEN PIZZAS

Makes 2 pan pizzas (12" each)

I've been making homemade pizzas for years, and barbecue chicken is a family favorite. The toppings for this one are unchanging: barbecue sauce (spicy for the grownups, a sweeter version for the kiddos), chicken, cilantro, and red onion with mozzarella cheese. It never fails.

Pizza dough, on the other hand, is a completely different story. I worked with many dough recipes throughout the years—knead, no knead, quick rise, long ferment, oil, no oil. Pans, pizza stones, grills . . . there are so many options to choose from, it can be downright mind-boggling.

Cast-iron skillets are great for making a beautiful pan pizza that's golden brown and oily on the bottom with a chewy crust. I've learned that my favorite dough for this is a no-knead recipe with a long ferment, not unlike the popular Dutch Oven Crusty Bread recipes on my blog, a method undeniably made famous by Jim Lahey. However, I got the idea to use a similar method for pizza dough in a cast-iron skillet from fellow blogger Rebecca Lindamood at *Foodie with Family,* and she got the inspiration from J. Kenji López-Alt, the managing culinary director at Serious Eats. Recipe attribution is a dynamic, complex thing. Food is a narrative that's always being written, and sometimes it's difficult to grab on to a phrase and say who authored it. But that doesn't mean we shouldn't try. When it comes to no-knead shaggy doughs mixed with wooden spoons and left undisturbed for a long rise, I think we will probably always circle back to Jim Lahey. All this is to say that this pizza dough recipe and method came from several brilliant sources all combining to make an exceptional pizza pie.

recipe continues

FOR THE DOUGH:

2½ cups "OO" flour, or other high-gluten bread flour

1½ teaspoons kosher salt

½ teaspoon instant yeast

2 teaspoons + 2 tablespoons extra-virgin olive oil, divided

1 cup + 3 tablespoons water

FOR THE TOPPINGS:

1 cup chopped cooked chicken breast

1¼ cups barbecue sauce, divided

Salt and ground black pepper

2 cups shredded mozzarella cheese

⅓ cup thinly sliced red onion

⅓ cup cilantro, chopped

1 *To make the dough:* In a very large mixing bowl, combine the flour, salt, yeast, 2 teaspoons of the olive oil, and the water. Stir with a wooden spoon until a shaggy dough forms. Do not knead the dough. Cover and allow to rise for 8 hours, or up to 24. The dough should rise substantially inside the bowl.

2 Carefully transfer the dough to a lightly floured work surface. Divide the dough in half and form 2 balls.

3 Grease two 12" cast-iron skillets with the remaining 2 tablespoons olive oil. Place a ball of dough into each pan, turning it to coat it entirely in oil on all sides. Using your palm, flatten the dough gently, pressing it out toward the edges of the pan. Don't worry about getting it perfect at this stage; it will cover the pan more easily after it rises. Cover the dough with a kitchen towel and allow it to rise for 2 hours on the countertop.

4 Preheat the oven to 550°F.

5 Using your fingertips, press the risen dough lightly to cover the bottom of the pan entirely.

6 *To make the toppings:* Place the chicken in a bowl. Pour in ¼ cup of the barbecue sauce and stir to coat. Season with salt and pepper to taste.

7 Divide the remaining 1 cup barbecue sauce evenly onto each of the pizzas. Sprinkle each pizza with 1 cup of the cheese. Evenly distribute the barbecue chicken between the 2 pizzas. Sprinkle each pizza liberally with the red onion and cilantro.

8 Bake for 15 minutes, or until golden brown on the bottom, bubbly, and fragrant. Carefully transfer the pizzas to a cutting board and allow them to rest for 5 minutes before slicing.

HUNTER'S PIE

Makes 6 servings

There is some debate over what these types of meat and vegetable dishes topped with a layer of mashed potato should be called. Shepherd's Pie is the most common title, but it originally earned its name because the pie was made with lamb or mutton, hence the shepherds. Cottage Pie is the name most often used when the filling is made with your everyday ground beef. The word "cottage" evokes the feeling of a cozy, oft-made meal made in a quaint neighborhood, an everyman's dish. Then there's Hunter's Pie, which is typically made with venison, but I think many game meats, like moose, fit the bill nicely. I like to use moose, so I named this one Hunter's Pie. But feel free to call it whatever seems most familiar to you and use the meat you have that is local and available, which is really what this dish is all about.

FOR THE POTATOES:
1¾ pounds russet potatoes, peeled and chopped

¼ cup butter, melted

¼ cup milk

1 egg yolk

½ teaspoon garlic powder

Salt

½ cup grated Cheddar cheese

FOR THE FILLING:
1 tablespoon vegetable oil

1 onion, chopped

2 carrots, chopped

2 cloves garlic, minced

2 teaspoons fresh rosemary, chopped

1½ pounds ground moose or lean ground beef

2 tablespoons all-purpose flour

1½ tablespoons tomato paste

1 tablespoon Worcestershire sauce

3 tablespoons ketchup

1 cup beef broth

½ cup peas

½ cup corn

Salt and ground black pepper

1 *To make the potatoes:* Place a pot of salted water over high heat and bring to a boil. Add the potatoes and boil for 12 minutes, or until tender. Drain. Transfer the potatoes to the bowl of a stand mixer fitted with the whip attachment. Turn the mixer on low and gradually add the butter, milk, egg yolk, and garlic powder to the potatoes. Increase the speed and whip for 30 seconds, or until fluffy. Season with salt to taste. Set aside.

2 Preheat the oven to 400°F.

recipe continues

3 *To make the filling:* In a large oven-proof skillet, heat the oil over medium heat. Cook the onion and carrots, stirring frequently, for 2 minutes. Stir in the garlic and rosemary and cook for 1 minute, or until fragrant. Add the meat and cook until browned. Sprinkle the flour over the top, stir to coat, and cook for 2 minutes. Add the tomato paste, Worcestershire sauce, ketchup, and beef broth and stir until combined. Bring the mixture to a simmer and cook for 2 minutes, or until it thickens. Remove the pan from the heat and stir in the peas and corn. Season with salt and pepper to taste.

4 Using a rubber spatula, spread the potato mixture evenly over top of the filling. Sprinkle the potatoes with the cheese. Bake for 25 minutes, or until the cheese is melted, the potatoes are heated through, and the filling is bubbling. Serve in bowls.

JALAPEÑO POPPER MACARONI AND CHEESE

Makes 6 servings

This flavorful stove-top macaroni and cheese recipe never makes a trip to the oven, so it remains perfectly creamy without drying out. For my jalapeño popper version, I've added a spicy jalapeño, cooling cream cheese, and some toasted panko bread crumbs on top for a little added crunch, reminiscent of a classic popper. It's comfort food with a kick.

3 cups water

1½ cups whole milk, divided

3 cups elbow macaroni

1 teaspoon salt, plus additional to taste

2 tablespoons butter

1 large jalapeño chile pepper, thinly sliced

2 teaspoons cornstarch

½ teaspoon garlic powder

3 cups grated sharp Cheddar cheese

3 ounces cream cheese

¼ cup panko bread crumbs, toasted

1 In a Dutch oven or large pot over high heat, stir together the water, 1 cup of the milk, the pasta, and salt. Bring to a boil, stirring often to prevent the pasta from sticking to the bottom of the pan. Reduce the heat to medium and simmer, continuing to stir often, for 9 minutes, or until the pasta is al dente.

2 Meanwhile, in a small skillet, melt the butter over medium-high heat. Cook the jalapeño pepper for 2 minutes, or until fragrant and tender. Turn off the heat and set aside.

3 In a small bowl, stir together the remaining ½ cup milk with the cornstarch and garlic powder. Add to the pasta mixture, stirring until it begins to thicken. Add the Cheddar and cream cheese and mix until creamy and smooth. If the mixture is too thick, gradually add more water to make it creamier. Add the jalapeño and butter and toss to combine. Season with more salt as needed. Sprinkle the top of the macaroni with the toasted panko and serve promptly while hot.

CHIPOTLE CHICKEN ENCHILADAS WITH ROASTED BUTTERNUT SQUASH AND BLACK BEANS

Makes 6 servings

Enchilada sauce from scratch is a breeze, and the flavor is out of this world. I used to make my popular huevos rancheros for brunch at the restaurant using a variation of this sauce. I had huevos rancheros regulars who would show up every week, sometimes requesting extra corn tortillas to sop up the sauce.

When making enchiladas at home, I love to simmer the chicken directly in the enchilada sauce to marry the flavors. When the chicken is tender and beginning to fall apart, I toss the meat into my Kitchen-Aid stand mixer and use the paddle attachment to shred the chicken. It takes about 60 seconds all told, and it's a lot less work than shredding it by hand.

FOR THE CHIPOTLE ENCHILADA SAUCE:

1 onion

1 chipotle pepper in adobo sauce

2 cloves garlic

2 tablespoons canola oil

1 tablespoon chili powder

1 tablespoon ground cumin

1½ teaspoons sugar

½ teaspoon salt

1 can (15 ounces) tomato sauce

2 cups water

1½ pounds boneless, skinless chicken breasts

1 cup peeled and finely cubed butternut squash

1 tablespoon vegetable oil

Salt and ground black pepper

1 cup black beans, rinsed and drained

½ cup sour cream

14 yellow corn tortillas, steamed (see note)

2 cups shredded Colby Jack cheese

¼ cup crumbled cotija cheese

FOR SERVING:

¼ cup sliced green onions

¼ cup cilantro, chopped

Sour cream

recipe continues

1 *To make the chipotle enchilada sauce:* Peel and quarter the onion. Add it to a food processor, along with the chipotle pepper and garlic. Process until finely chopped.

2 In a Dutch oven, heat the canola oil over medium heat. Cook the onion mixture, stirring frequently, for 90 seconds, or until tender and fragrant. Stir in the chili powder, cumin, sugar, and salt. Toast the spices for 90 seconds. Pour in the tomato sauce and water, stir to combine, and bring to a simmer. Add the chicken, cover, and simmer for 30 minutes, or until tender.

3 Meanwhile, preheat the oven to 400°F. Line a small rimmed baking sheet with foil. Place the butternut squash on the pan, drizzle with the oil, and season with salt and black pepper to taste. Roast for 12 to 15 minutes, or until tender and beginning to caramelize. Set aside.

4 Turn off the heat on the stove and remove the chicken from the sauce, reserving the sauce for assembling the enchiladas. Transfer the chicken to the mixing bowl of a stand mixer fitted with the paddle attachment and shred.

5 Increase the oven temperature to 425°F. Grease a 13" x 9" baking dish.

6 In a mixing bowl, combine the chicken, butternut squash, black beans, and sour cream. Stir together and season with salt to taste. Add ⅔ cup of the enchilada sauce to the filling to moisten it, stirring to combine.

7 Spoon ¼ cup of the chicken filling onto the center of a warm tortilla, roll it up, and place seam side down in the baking dish. Repeat until all of the filling and tortillas have been used. Coat the enchiladas with cooking spray and bake for 10 minutes, or until they begin to turn golden brown on the edges. (This helps the tortillas firm up and keep some of their texture when baked in the sauce.) Remove the pan from the oven and pour the enchilada sauce evenly over the enchiladas. Sprinkle with the Colby Jack and cotija cheeses. Bake for 20 minutes, or until the sauce is bubbling and the cheese is melted.

8 To serve, sprinkle the enchiladas with the green onions and cilantro. Serve with sour cream on the side.

NOTE: For easier enchilada assembly, I recommend steaming your corn tortillas in a tortilla warmer to make them more pliable before filling them.

ALASKA HOT DOGS WITH HARD CIDER CARAMELIZED ONIONS

Makes 4

Alaska is well known for its reindeer hot dogs. There used to be a famous hot dog cart in Anchorage where the owner served reindeer dogs slathered in caramelized onions deglazed with Coca-Cola. My version is a nod to that nostalgic local favorite, with onions cooked in hard cider, served with robust grainy mustard and a dill pickle spear. If you don't have access to reindeer hot dogs, a substantial locally made hot dog or bratwurst would be a fantastic substitute. Save some cider to drink with your dogs.

3 tablespoons butter

1 large onion (such as Vidalia), sliced

Salt and ground black pepper

½ cup hard apple cider

4 reindeer hot dogs or bratwurst

4 hot dog buns, toasted

Grainy mustard

4 dill pickle spears

1 In a skillet, melt the butter over medium heat. Add the onion, spreading the slices out so they make direct contact with the pan. Season generously with salt and pepper. Cook, stirring often, for 15 minutes, or until tender, golden, and beginning to caramelize. Deglaze the pan with the hard cider. Cook for 5 to 10 minutes, or until the alcohol has cooked out and the mixture has thickened. Keep warm.

2 Meanwhile, cook the hot dogs or bratwurst on the grill or in a hot skillet until cooked through in the center and browned on the exterior.

3 To assemble the hot dogs, lay each cooked hot dog inside a warm bun. Top with a generous heap of cider onions. Drizzle each dog with grainy mustard and top each with a pickle spear.

SHEET PAN BALSAMIC CHICKEN WITH BRUSSELS SPROUTS AND SWEET POTATOES

Makes 4 servings

Sheet pan meals are amazing. They have been growing in popularity because you can toss all of your dinner components—protein, vegetables, and starch—onto 1 pan and roast them all together. The vegetables get caramelized, the potatoes get tender, and the meat or poultry gets juicy and delicious all at once. Sheet pan recipes can be lifesavers for busy families who are looking for an easy, well-rounded meal with lots of color and flavor with a lot less cleanup afterward.

3 tablespoons extra-virgin olive oil, divided

¼ cup balsamic vinegar

1 tablespoon Dijon mustard

1 tablespoon honey

1 clove garlic, minced

2 teaspoons fresh rosemary, chopped

Kosher salt and freshly cracked black pepper

1¼ pounds boneless, skinless chicken thighs

1 pound Brussels sprouts, trimmed and quartered

1 cup peeled and cubed sweet potatoes, (cubed about the same size as the quartered Brussels sprouts)

½ cup roughly chopped red onion

1 In a small bowl, combine 2 tablespoons of the olive oil, the vinegar, mustard, honey, garlic, rosemary, and a generous amount of salt and pepper. Mix well. Place the chicken thighs in a resealable plastic bag.

2 Pour two-thirds of the balsamic mixture over the chicken to coat. Seal the bag and place it in the refrigerator to marinate for at least 1 hour.

3 Preheat the oven to 425°F. On a large rimmed sheet pan, scatter the Brussels sprouts, sweet potatoes, and onion.

Drizzle the remaining 1 tablespoon olive oil over the vegetables. Season with salt and pepper to taste. Toss to coat. Drizzle the remaining one-third of the balsamic mixture over the vegetables and toss again. Remove the chicken thighs from the marinade and place them on the sheet pan, nestling them in between the vegetables.

4 Roast for 25 minutes, or until the vegetables are caramelized and tender, a thermometer inserted in the thickest portion of a thigh registers 165°F, and the juices run clear.

5 / CHEERS TO ALASKA
BEVERAGES

BEVERAGES

T was a coffee drinker first, before anything else. My senior year of high school, I took a full load of courses at the community college 20 minutes outside of town. I took classes like Creative Writing, Shakespeare, and Eastern Religions, staying far away from math and science courses, which have never been my strong suit. Bleh. Numbers. I'm a word girl. I especially remember a remarkably difficult World Civilizations course with a stellar female professor and heavy writing component. Although I considered myself a competent writer by that point, I was still young, and the course stretched and challenged me. I loved it. I drank it up.

Just outside the World Civ class, there was an espresso bar. One day, I was feeling particularly foggy as I headed into my hardest class. I had some spare change in my pocket, so I stopped to grab a vanilla latte on my way in. After that I was hooked. My coffee addiction was born. Sweet espresso drinks like caramel macchiatos and iced mint mochas would become vital to my surviving the 4 years of university to follow, maintaining two jobs, and being a resident assistant.

When college was over, my coffee addiction held fast, although by now I had a drip coffeepot on my counter and kept a bottle of creamer in the refrigerator. Coffee was with me through all of the sleepless nights as a young mother, the ear infections, the emergency room visits, the hospital stays. I was 23 when my oldest son, Brady, was born, followed by my middle son, Connor, 21 months later. And finally, my daughter, Kelty, almost exactly 3 years after that. I can't tell you how I stayed afloat those years except to say that there was always coffee. By that time in California, there was a drive-thru Starbucks on just about every corner, and those prolific cafés were this young mom's best friend. With children strapped safely in car seats, listening to The Wiggles, at least one of them crying at any given time, I was able to fuel up on coffee without ever having to get anyone out of the car.

So you can imagine that when we moved to Alaska, one of the biggest shocks to my system was that there was no longer a Starbucks on every corner. There wasn't a corner. Or even a city nearby to speak of. Instead, there was snow and endless trees, and a long stretch of highway headed north for miles, ending abruptly in a wilderness with no cell phone signal. We had a tiny post office. A gas station. One elementary school and one combination middle-high school, far out and tucked away in the trees. More snow. Moose. Icy ocean views. Steaming snow-capped volcanoes across the water. The nearest Starbucks was more than an hour away round trip by car, tucked inside of a grocery store, without a drive-thru.

I quickly realized that I had been downright spoiled in California. In hindsight, I laugh at myself for this. If I wanted a simpler lifestyle by moving to Alaska, I was going to have to embrace the lack of those conveniences upon which I'd come to rely. If I wanted a pumpkin spice latte, I was going to have to make it my damn self. It became one of my first recipes on the blog, along with coffee creamers made from scratch, and homemade cold brew in Mason jars. What at first seemed like a loss was ultimately a tremendous gain. Through sheer isolation, Alaska afforded me the time, perspective, and lack of resources to begin cooking more from scratch, making things myself to which I didn't otherwise have access, and becoming a more self-reliant cook and human being. Naturally, these things made feeding my family much more affordable and much more wholesome at the same time. The slower pace of life in Alaska also allowed me to pursue my neglected passions, such as writing, photography, and food. It's out of these things that *Alaska from Scratch* was born. Cheers to Alaska, indeed.

Cocktails, on the other hand, are a completely different story. I didn't have my first drink until I was well into my thirties, years after my mother passed. I had spent many nights of my childhood in dark dive bars, shooting pool, eating bar nuts and Maraschino cherries, and playing "The Devil Went Down to Georgia" on the jukebox. In elementary school, I had the phone numbers to all the local bars memorized and would call them at night when my mother didn't come home.

After spending most of my life downright terrified of alcohol and, more specifically, alcoholism, I found this was one of those things that shifted in me and eventually fell away after my mother died. It was another one of the ways I had shaped my life as a reaction against things that had happened in my childhood, and it was no longer necessary or helpful. I'm not sure it ever was. It took me a while to convince myself I would be able to drink in moderation and to muster the courage to try even a single drink. As it turns out, with this and with much of life, I am much stronger than I realize.

At first, I was an extremely tentative drinker, taking just a sip of a fine wine pairing with an entrée to round out the meal. I was timid about going into the alcoholic beverages section of the store to purchase drinks for cooking and recipe testing. I would feel like a stranger there, and I was afraid people would see me with bottles in my cart. I didn't have the foggiest idea what to order off the wine list and was afraid of looking uninformed in the food world. It takes bravery and constant, deliberate work to conquer our fears, and this was a huge one of mine. Today, when I make a cocktail at home or order a hard cider with my buffalo wings while watching a hockey game at the sports bar, my wife and I casually clink glasses. She and I both know that underneath the sound is a quiet celebration of freedom from former fears that held us both down.

FRESH MINT ICED MOCHA

Makes 2 servings

Mint iced mochas take me back to the little café we had in college. I'd stop there several times a week for a much-needed caffeine infusion on humid, sunny San Diego days. There was something about the jolt of the mint against the chill of the ice that reinvigorated me every time. Of course, those mint mochas were made with bottles of unnaturally green mint-flavored syrup that more resembled a bottle of cough syrup than anything else. But I loved them.

If you haven't tried fresh mint in your coffee, now is the time. It's subtle and herbaceous and complex all at once. It will make you ponder every sip, tasting the nuances. You'll want to keep going back for more. And the hint of chocolate anchors the whole thing. Feel free to play around with the ratio of coffee to milk to syrup in this recipe until it's just the way you like it.

FOR THE MINT MOCHA SIMPLE SYRUP:

½ cup water

½ cup sugar

½ cup fresh mint leaves, roughly chopped

½ teaspoon unsweetened cocoa powder

½ teaspoon vanilla extract

FOR THE ICED COFFEE:

Chocolate syrup (optional)

Ice cubes

1 cup milk

1½ cups cold coffee (cold brew works well here)

1 *To make the mint mocha simple syrup:* In a small saucepan over medium heat, stir together the water and sugar until the sugar is dissolved. Bring the mixture to a simmer. Add the mint leaves, cocoa, and vanilla and stir until the cocoa is incorporated. Remove the pan from the heat and allow the mint leaves to steep for 15 minutes. Strain through a fine-mesh sieve. Chill until ready to serve.

2 *To make the iced coffee:* If desired, squirt chocolate syrup around the inside of 2 tall glasses. Fill the glasses with ice cubes. Divide the milk between the glasses. Top each with the coffee. Sweeten each glass with 2 tablespoons of the mint mocha syrup, or to taste. Stir to combine.

3 Any leftover mint mocha syrup can be refrigerated in a sealed container and saved for up to 7 days.

VANILLA BEAN COFFEE CREAMER

Makes 3 cups

I have been sporting a ridiculous coffee creamer obsession for years. I can't drink my drip coffee or French press without it. And it's not just a splash. It's a copious glug glug. When I got to Alaska, flavored store-bought creamers were much more expensive, and the grocery store was much farther away. It took only 1 horrendous morning of waking up to not a drop of creamer in the house before I began developing my own homemade coffee creamer recipes and posting them on the blog. I especially enjoyed making the harder-to-find seasonal flavors like pumpkin spice, peppermint mocha, and eggnog. But vanilla is the flavor we enjoy most often, year-round.

¾ cup sugar

¾ cup water

1 vanilla bean

1 teaspoon vanilla extract

2 cups half-and-half

In a saucepan over medium-high heat, combine the sugar and water. Stir until the sugar is dissolved and the mixture begins to simmer. Add the vanilla bean and remove the pan from the heat. Allow the vanilla bean to steep for 10 minutes. Remove the vanilla bean to a cutting board. Using a small, sharp knife, slice the vanilla bean pod down the side and scrape out the caviar. Add the caviar to the simple syrup, stirring to disperse. Stir in the vanilla extract. Refrigerate for 30 minutes, or until chilled through. Measure 1 cup of the vanilla bean simple syrup and add it to the half-and-half, stirring to combine. Store the creamer in the refrigerator in an airtight container, such as a large Mason jar, for up to 1 week. Shake or stir before each use. Use as desired to flavor and sweeten your coffee.

TOASTED COCONUT COFFEE CREAMER

Makes 3 cups

Here's an island take on my classic creamer recipe, a refreshing treat for warmer days. Try adding it to iced cold brew coffee. Maybe throw a cocktail umbrella on top and dream of white sand beaches and coral reefs while you're at it.

¾ cup sugar

¾ cup water

½ cup coconut, toasted

½ teaspoon vanilla extract

¼ teaspoon coconut extract

2 cups half-and-half

In a saucepan over medium-high heat, combine the sugar and water. Stir until the sugar is dissolved and the mixture begins to simmer. Add the toasted coconut and remove the pan from the heat. Allow the coconut to steep for 10 minutes. Stir in the vanilla and coconut extracts. Strain through a fine-mesh sieve. Measure 1 cup of the coconut simple syrup and add it to the half-and-half, stirring to combine. Store the creamer in the refrigerator in an airtight container, such as a large Mason jar, for up to 1 week. Use as desired to flavor and sweeten your coffee.

LONDON FOG

Makes 1 serving

Whether I've spent the morning writing, cooking, spending time
with the kids, or all of the above, I usually need a second infusion of caffeine
in the midafternoon. Rather than brewing more coffee or driving to a café,
my beverage of choice is a London Fog—sweetened Earl Grey tea with milk
and vanilla. I've tried many variations, but my favorite is to make it
with frothy half-and-half and fragrant vanilla bean paste.

I'm typically not one for kitchen gadgets, but I love my handy dandy
battery-operated milk frother, a tool to which I was introduced by my Uncle Will
and Aunt Claudette. It's a delightful miniature whisk-like thing that allows you to
froth your beverages without having to run an espresso machine or steam milk.
Just make sure you fully submerge it into your beverage before turning it on;
otherwise, you'll splatter yourself and likely your kitchen, too.

If you can't get your hands on vanilla bean paste (I often order
mine on Amazon because it can be hard to find here), split a vanilla bean
and scrape ¼ teaspoon of vanilla bean caviar for the same result. The
tiny black flecks of vanilla are irresistible swirling in the creamy
half-and-half. You won't regret the little bit of extra effort.

1 Earl Grey tea bag

1 cup boiling water

¼ cup half-and-half

2 teaspoons sugar

¼ teaspoon vanilla bean
paste (or ¼ teaspoon caviar
from a vanilla bean)

To a 12-ounce mug, add the tea bag. Pour the boiling water over the tea bag and allow to steep for 2 minutes. In another 12-ounce mug, combine the half-and-half, sugar, and vanilla bean paste. Froth or steam the half-and-half mixture until about doubled in volume. Pour the cream mixture into the tea. Stir gently to combine, being careful not to disturb the froth. Serve promptly.

RHUBARB ICED TEA WITH ROSEMARY AND CARDAMOM

Makes 1 pitcher

Rhubarb is one of our most treasured local ingredients here in Alaska. The natural acidity of rhubarb plays nicely in iced tea, almost mimicking citrus. It also lends a lovely millennial pink hue to the simple syrup. Combining it with the woodiness of fresh rosemary and a hint of aromatic cardamom makes this iced tea as complex as it is refreshing. To save time, I like to use cold brew tea bags, which steep in cold water in only 10 minutes. But if you're the type of person who likes to let their iced tea come to full flavor by steeping all day in the sunshine, don't skip this recipe. Just make a batch of the rhubarb simple syrup and add it to your pitcher of iced tea when it's ready.

2 quarts (8 cups) cold water

3 cold brew iced tea bags

4 cups ice cubes

Fresh rosemary sprigs, for garnish

FOR THE SIMPLE SYRUP:

1/2 cup sugar

1/2 cup water

1/8 teaspoon cardamom

3/4 cup thinly sliced rhubarb

1 sprig fresh rosemary

1 Pour the cold water into a tall pitcher. Steep the cold brew tea bags in the pitcher of water for 10 minutes. Meanwhile, prepare the simple syrup.

2 *To make the simple syrup:* In a small saucepan over medium heat, combine the sugar, water, and cardamom. Stir until the sugar is dissolved and the mixture begins to simmer. Add the rhubarb and rosemary. Simmer for 3 minutes. Remove from the heat and allow the syrup to cool.

3 Strain the simple syrup using a fine-mesh sieve. Add the syrup to the pitcher of tea, stirring to combine. Discard the tea bags. Serve over the ice with fresh rosemary sprigs.

BLUEBERRY BASIL LEMONADE

Makes 4 to 6 servings

Wild blueberries grow all over the Kenai Peninsula and in several other parts of Alaska in late summer. Many families have their favorite berry-picking spots, often making a day of it to hike in and gather baskets and baskets full of them. But you have to take great caution because the black bears enjoy the blueberries even more than we humans do! While a lot of the blueberry haul ends up in the freezer or preserved in homemade batches of jam, I love to use a few fresh ones to toast to the end of summer with a glass of this pucker-worthy, herbaceous blueberry lemonade.

FOR THE SIMPLE SYRUP:
¾ cup sugar
¾ cup water

FOR THE LEMONADE:
1 cup freshly squeezed lemon juice
1 quart (4 cups) cold water
⅓ cup fresh blueberries, muddled
2 tablespoons fresh basil, cut into a chiffonade

FOR SERVING:
Ice cubes
1 lemon, sliced
Small whole basil leaves
Fresh blueberries

1 *To make the simple syrup:* In a small saucepan over medium heat, combine the sugar and water. Stir until the mixture is heated through and the sugar has dissolved. Set the simple syrup aside to cool.

2 *To make the lemonade:* In a mixing bowl, combine the lemon juice, cold water, blueberries, and basil. Stir in the simple syrup. Chill the lemonade in the refrigerator for at least 30 minutes. When ready to serve, pour the lemonade through a fine-mesh sieve into a pitcher.

3 To serve, fill tall glasses with ice, lemon slices, basil leaves, and blueberries as desired. Pour the chilled lemonade over the ice and serve promptly.

CASHEW HORCHATA

Makes 2 quarts (8 cups)

Spending many of my early years in Southern California not only
gave me an inexplicable affection for Mexican cuisine, but also for Mexican
tamarind candies from the ice cream truck, Mexican paletas from a hand-pushed
cart with a jingle bell, and creamy horchata from the agua fresca dispensers in
restaurants and convenience stores. I have a hard time enjoying a plate of street
tacos without a tall, icy glass of cinnamon-laden horchata close by.

If you're not familiar with horchata, there are several versions of the milky white
beverage, depending on whether you're enjoying a glass in Spain, Latin American,
or the United States. Some varieties incorporate almonds or cashews, others rice,
and still others seeds. The version I grew up drinking in Southern California was
most often made with white rice and cinnamon sticks, spiked with vanilla.

Authentic horchata isn't easy to find in Alaska, so I worked hard to develop
a recipe to replicate one of the most refreshing flavors of my childhood.
A good, strong blender will make quick work of this. But if you don't have one,
soaking your cashews and rice in water for 4 hours will do the trick.

| 1 cup raw cashews | 8 cups cold water, divided | 5 cinnamon sticks |
| 1 cup uncooked white rice | 2 tablespoons vanilla extract | 10 ounces sweetened condensed milk, divided |

1 In a mixing bowl, combine the cashews and rice. Cover with water and set aside to soak for 4 hours.

NOTE: If you have a high-powered blender like a Vitamix, you can skip the soaking step.

2 Drain the cashews and rice and transfer them to a blender. Add 4 cups of the cold water, the vanilla, cinnamon sticks, and 5 ounces of the sweetened condensed milk. Blend on medium-high speed for 90 seconds, or until the rice, cashews, and cinnamon sticks are processed to a fine meal. Transfer the liquid to a pitcher, reserving the solids at the bottom. Add the remaining 4 cups water and 5 ounces sweetened condensed milk to the blender with the rice solids. Whirl for 60 to 90 seconds. If you like your horchata sweeter, add extra sweetened condensed milk. Transfer the liquid to the pitcher. If you like your horchata to be smooth, strain it through a fine-mesh sieve. Chill.

HORCHATA RUM PUNCH

Makes 1 serving

My homemade horchata recipe makes a terrific cocktail with the
addition of some dark spiced rum, a from-scratch version
of the bottled Rumchata found in many beverage shops.

4 ounces Cashew Horchata
(page 168)

1½ ounces dark rum

Cinnamon stick

Fill an old fashioned glass with ice. In a cocktail shaker, combine the horchata and rum. Shake vigorously. Pour over the ice and serve with a cinnamon stick on top.

THE GINNY WEASLEY

Makes 1 serving

The cocktail of choice at our house is almost always a variation
on the Moscow mule—spicy ginger beer, freshly squeezed lime juice, and
vodka served up in copper mugs. It's a sentimental favorite because I tried
my first mule while my wife and I were on a date at a pub called Harbor
Town. She recommended it to me and was sure I'd love it because of my
affinity for all things involving ginger and lime. She knows me well.

At home, we love to substitute dark rum for the vodka, which quickly
transforms a mule into what's known as a Dark 'n Stormy. But, since my wife
and I are both gin lovers, our favorite version is what we like to call a Ginny.

One weekend we went for a quick Valentine's Day getaway to the tiny
historic mining village of Hope, Alaska. Before we got on the road to this remote
place in the dead of winter, I made sure I had packed a lime, a bottle of ginger
beer, and some good British gin to make Ginnys when we arrived at the cabin.
Incidentally, I also happened to have a blood orange on hand to slice up for
breakfast the next morning. Inspiration struck, and I added blood orange
juice to our usual Ginny recipe, which caused the drinks to take on a magical
red hue. We affectionately dubbed the cocktail The Ginny Weasley because,
like the Harry Potter character, the drink has elements of depth and mystery
and romance. And, of course, that trademark gingery red coloring.

4 ounces spicy ginger beer (our favorites are Cock 'n Bull or Goslings)	1½ ounces gin (such as Plymouth) ½ lime	½ tablespoon blood orange juice

Fill a copper mug with cubed ice. Pour
the ginger beer over the ice, followed
by the gin. Squeeze the lime half into
the cocktail, dropping the squeezed
lime shell into the mug when finished.
Finish the drink with the blood orange
juice. Stir well and serve promptly.

GRAPEFRUIT JALAPEÑO MARGARITA

Makes 1 serving

It was my dear longtime friend Jacob who first introduced me to the sheer perfection that is a jalapeño margarita one summer evening in San Diego's historic Balboa Park. He ordered it casually, on the rocks, as he seemingly often did. When the drink came to the table, I reached for his glass and tried it. I was enamored by the saltiness of the rim, the fresh, sour lime, the subtle sweetness of the simple syrup, and the way the heat from the tequila and the jalapeño dance together at the back of the palate. I turned to my wife (who was then my girlfriend) and said, "You've got to try this."

We now often enjoy jalapeño margaritas at home in Alaska. During citrus season, I love to add grapefruit, which brings a welcome bitter note. And finally, I put a smoky hint of chili powder into the salt on the rim as a finishing touch. It tastes like San Diego in a glass, and it's ideal paired with some authentic Baja-style Mexican food.

2 ounces reposado tequila

2 ounces freshly squeezed grapefruit juice (pink or ruby red)

1 ounce lime juice

¾ ounce simple syrup, or to taste

¼ ounce Cointreau

5 jalapeño chile pepper slices, divided

1 tablespoon kosher salt

½ teaspoon chili powder

1 lime wedge

1 In a cocktail shaker, combine the tequila, grapefruit juice, lime juice, simple syrup, Cointreau, and 2 jalapeño pepper slices. Shake vigorously over ice until thoroughly chilled and combined.

2 In a small bowl, stir together the salt and chili powder. Rub the rim of a short highball glass with the lime wedge, then dip the rim into the chili salt, coating it generously. Carefully place ice cubes into the highball glass, being careful not to disturb the salt on the rim. Pour the cocktail over the ice and add the remaining 3 jalapeño pepper slices to the glass. Serve.

NOTE: This cocktail gets spicier toward the end of the drink. It's part of the fun.

CHAI HOT TODDY

Makes 4 servings

My friend Jacob is quite the jet-setter, so when he came to Alaska for Christmas one year, he came to hibernate and reboot. For his visit, our list of to-do's during the darkest, coldest time of the year was: wear cozies, binge-watch Netflix, write Christmas postcards, snuggle under blankets, wrap presents, and drink hot toddies. Hot toddies have long been thought to not only warm you up from the inside out but also to have healing qualities to soothe those winter colds and flus. Jacob made a magical concoction he called broth that steeped on the stove for hours and filled the house with the coziest smell imaginable. This broth became the base for his hot toddies—a perfect mixture of honey, lemon, Chai tea, and whole spices. Grab a sturdy mug, add a shot of bourbon, kick your feet up, and settle in.

2 cups water

2 Chai tea bags

¼ cup honey

2 cinnamon sticks

3 whole cloves

3 lemon slices

4 shots bourbon

1 In a small saucepan over low heat, combine the water, tea bags, honey, cinnamon sticks, cloves, and lemon slices. Stir to dissolve the honey. When the mixture is hot, remove the pan from the heat. Allow the mixture to steep for 15 minutes. The liquid should be a deep amber color, fragrant, and steaming. Remove and discard the tea bags and cloves. Keep hot.

2 To make a hot toddy, add a ladle of the hot Chai mixture to a mug. Top with a shot of bourbon. Serve with a cinnamon stick or lemon slice, if desired. Add more honey as desired to sweeten to taste.

SPARKLING ELDERFLOWER ROSÉ

Makes 2 servings

Of the many things for which I have to thank my friend Kim Sunée, one of them is introducing me to the magic of bubbles with a splash of elderflower liqueur. It's joy in a glass. When I'm feeling particularly festive and maybe even a little sophisticated, for holidays, celebrations, or weddings, this has become my beverage of choice. I add a squeeze of lemon and a slice of cucumber to awaken the palate to all of the memorable moments worth toasting. Cheers.

6 ounces brut rosé
1 ounce St. Germain

1 tablespoon lemon juice
4 dashes bitters

2 cucumber slices

Select 2 champagne flutes or short cocktail glasses. Divide the brut rosé between the glasses. Add half of the St. Germain and half of the lemon juice to each. Add 2 dashes of bitters to each glass. Serve each with a slice of cucumber.

NOTE: Also lovely over ice.

APEROL SPRITZ

Makes 2 servings

It's always exciting for me to add new cocktails to my drink vocabulary. I tasted my first Aperol Spritz at an Italian restaurant in iconic Grand Central Terminal in New York City. Prior to that, I had never seen the drink, having never been to Italy myself, where it is apparently quite popular, particularly in the summer months. Aperol is an apéritif with a bright, enchanting hue, swirling with bitter orange, floral notes, and rhubarb. It's added to bubbly Prosecco and club soda to make an effervescent and refreshing cocktail.

The week after I returned home to Alaska after my trip to New York City, an article landed in my inbox about food trends for foodie travelers. The Aperol Spritz was named the up-and-coming cocktail of choice, with searches for the drink up 97 percent on Pinterest. Had I not just traveled to NYC, I wouldn't have known what an Aperol Spritz was. Now I make these at home and am doing my part to put this summery Italian cocktail on the map here in Alaska.

10 ounces Prosecco
4 ounces Aperol

2 ounces club soda or seltzer water

Orange slices

Add ice to 2 large stemmed wine glasses. Divide the Prosecco between the glasses. Add half of the Aperol to each. Finish by adding half of the club soda or seltzer water to each and topping each with an orange slice.

NOTE: More or less Aperol can be added to taste, depending on how sweet you like your cocktails. You can also play around with your Aperol Spritz by adding grapefruit or passionfruit juices to the mix, using a splash of your favorite bitters, or substituting a sparkling rosé in place of the Prosecco.

6/ BAKED ALASKA
DESSERTS

DESSERTS

I've undergone quite the evolution in my life when it comes to cakes. My mother would sometimes decorate cakes for birthdays when I was little. Somewhere along the way, before I was born, she had attended some cake decorating classes, and she took great pride in her frosting skills and her creativity. She would ask me which flavor of boxed cake mix I wanted, whip it up, and then painstakingly decorate it with lots of different frosting colors, using pastry bags and a whole assortment of tips she kept in a kit. I remember thinking the kit was really cool. She would often find a cake pan shaped like a cartoon character, like Cookie Monster or one of the Care Bears, then use a tiny star tip to pipe stars all over the cake to create the character. She also knew how to make flowers out of frosting, which I still to this day find impressive and have no idea how to do. I can't for the life of me recall ever seeing her decorate the cakes with my own eyes. She always wanted there to be a big reveal, so she kept them a secret. I never learned how to do it.

When I became a young mom, although I had no cake-decorating experience whatsoever, I began making cupcakes every year for each of my three children's birthdays. I would select the birthday cupcake recipes weeks and sometimes even months in advance. I remember every flavor of cake, every color of frosting, every coordinating paper cup, and every decoration, sprinkle, and candle I've used for each one. I can see that I probably got this from my mother.

When the special moment came, I would place the candles just so, turn off the lights, light the candles, and grab my camera just as we began to sing "Happy Birthday." I love capturing the excitement that flickers in my children's eyes—that anticipation that builds as they ready themselves to blow out their candles and take that first bite. And even more than that, I love looking back on all the birthday photos to see how they've grown and changed, and how each dessert reflects their personality from that moment in time.

I didn't make cupcakes because they were uber-trendy, although they were exploding in popularity at that time. I made them because they were easier and less intimidating than layer cakes. Cupcakes felt doable to me as a busy mom with three young kids. But, not long after we moved to Alaska and I became a food blogger, my oldest son, Brady, declared that he had grown too old for cupcakes and wanted a full-size layer cake for his birthday.

Eeeeek!

Say whaaaattttt?!

Noooooooo.

<Insert horrified emoji face here.>

My days as a cupcake baker were numbered, and I was going to have to put on my big cake pants. I was terrified. Layer cakes were scary. What if the cake broke as I was trying to get it out of the pan? What would I do if the cake came out lopsided or if my attempts at frosting and decorating the cake were catastrophic? There would be crying and tears—all mine—and there would be family photographs kept for all of time to immortalize my cake-baking failures.

I agonized over that first cake, researching recipes and methods. I had to arm myself with new equipment, like a rotating cake decorating stand and offset spatulas (which I now love and adore). Because Brady's favorite color at that time was green and because he loves all things citrus, I tried my hand at a Key lime cake with cream cheese frosting, decorated using an ombré frosting technique. Although the cake wasn't perfect, it turned out really well—tender and tangy and blog-worthy even—and it gave me the confidence I needed to make more layer cakes in the future.

After I conquered my cake-baking fears, all three children began requesting "big cakes" for their birthdays each year. The more I practiced, the better I got, and I soon even began to enjoy the process. I started to collect reliable cake recipes because there's no confidence boost in the kitchen like having a solid recipe upon which to rely. My absolute favorite cake, both to bake and to eat, is Beatty's Chocolate Cake by Ina Garten. In my mind, it's the perfect cake, and it has never once failed me. I love the gorgeous chocolate frosting recipe she includes with it, but I've also decorated it with other frostings, too, from peanut butter to peppermint marshmallow to Oreo buttercream. It's always intoxicatingly moist and deeply chocolatey. I can't say enough good things about that recipe.

Cake baking is a labor of love. When I make a cake for family or friends, I cream my wishes into that sugar and butter. I pour their personalities into the batter like buttermilk. I whip my hopes into those lofty egg whites. I breathe my wisdom into the cloud of confectioners' sugar that rises up and dusts the entire kitchen and anyone nearby. I spread my affection on with the frosting, in generous swoops. And when the cake is made and there is nothing left but piles of mixing bowls and spatulas and pastry bags, I remember that life, like cake making, is both messy and beautiful.

COCONUT LAYER CAKE WITH COCONUT PASTRY CREAM FILLING

Makes up to 12 servings

This stunning cake is a complete showstopper for special occasions such as a wintry holiday party, a bridal shower, or a birthday bash. The coconut pastry cream filling can be made a day or 2 in advance to simplify the process. The cake layers can also be made in advance and chilled, which makes for easier handling and decorating. However, be sure to allow time to let the cake come back to room temperature before serving, because that's when the flavor and texture are at their peak.

FOR THE COCONUT PASTRY CREAM FILLING:
1 can (13.5 ounces) unsweetened coconut milk
3/4 cup granulated sugar
1 tablespoon vanilla extract
Pinch of salt
3 large egg yolks
2 tablespoons cornstarch
2 tablespoons butter
1 cup shredded coconut

FOR THE CAKE:
1 cup butter, softened
2 cups granulated sugar
5 eggs, separated
2 cups cake flour
1 teaspoon baking soda
2 cups shredded coconut
1 cup buttermilk
3/4 cup unsweetened coconut milk
1 teaspoon vanilla extract
1 teaspoon coconut extract

1/2 teaspoon almond extract
1/2 teaspoon salt

FOR THE FROSTING:
1 package (8 ounces) cream cheese, softened
1/2 cup butter, softened
1 teaspoon vanilla extract
1/2 teaspoon coconut extract
1/2 teaspoon almond extract
3 3/4 cups confectioners' sugar

1 *To make the coconut pastry cream filling:* In a saucepan, heat the coconut milk, granulated sugar, vanilla, and salt over medium heat. In a bowl, whisk together the egg yolks and cornstarch. Slowly whisk 1/2 cup of the hot coconut milk mixture into the egg yolk mixture to temper the eggs. Pour the egg yolk mixture into the pan of coconut milk mixture and whisk to combine. Increase the heat to medium high and cook, whisking constantly, for 3 minutes, or until the mixture thickens and bubbles. Whisk in the butter. If there are lumps, strain the pastry cream through a fine-mesh sieve. Stir in the coconut. Pour the curd into a shallow dish, cover with plastic wrap, and refrigerate. This can be made 1 to 2 days ahead.

recipe continues

2 *To make the cake:* Preheat the oven to 350°F. Grease and flour three 9" round cake pans. Line the bottom of each pan with a round of parchment paper the same size as the pan.

3 In the bowl of a stand mixer fitted with the paddle attachment, cream together the butter and granulated sugar for 2 to 3 minutes, or until light and fluffy. Gradually add the egg yolks, beating until combined and scraping the sides of the bowl as needed.

4 In a mixing bowl, stir together the flour, baking soda, and coconut until just combined.

5 In a separate bowl, stir together the buttermilk, coconut milk, and extracts.

6 With the mixer on low speed, alternate adding the flour mixture with the buttermilk mixture in 3 stages, beginning with the flour, then buttermilk, then flour, then buttermilk, then finishing with the flour. Scrape the sides and bottom of the bowl as needed to ensure the ingredients are well incorporated.

7 In another bowl, beat the egg whites together with the salt until they form stiff peaks. With a rubber spatula, gently fold the egg whites into the batter until combined.

8 Evenly spread the batter into the cake pans, leveling them off with a large offset spatula. Bake for 25 to 30 minutes, or until set. Cool on wire racks before turning the cakes out of the pans and removing the parchment paper.

NOTE: The cakes are fragile, so chilling them in the fridge for a bit will help firm them up before you turn them out. They are also easier to frost when cold. But be sure to bring the cake back to room temperature for serving.

9 *To make the frosting:* In a large mixing bowl, cream together the cream cheese and butter until smooth. Add the extracts and mix to combine. Gradually add the confectioners' sugar. Beat on high speed for 1 minute, or until fluffy.

10 To assemble the cake, once the cake layers are cool, place the first layer on a cake plate or serving plate. Pipe a thick circle of frosting just around the top edge of the cake to hold in the pastry cream filling. Spread a layer of coconut pastry cream inside the circle of frosting. Top it with another layer of cake. Repeat with a circle of frosting and a layer of pastry cream. Top it with the third layer of cake. Frost the top and sides of the cake generously with the frosting. If desired, sprinkle the cake with shredded coconut. Serve at room temperature.

CHOCOLATE MINT EARTHQUAKE CAKE

Makes 8 to 10 servings

One of the things Alaska is known for are its earthquakes. There is an average of 1,000 earthquakes in the state each month, and we feel them frequently here on the Kenai Peninsula. The largest earthquake I've experienced in my lifetime was here in 2016, a magnitude 7.1 that was prolonged and jolting. And of course, there is the famous Great Alaska Earthquake of 1964, a whopping 9.2 magnitude, the largest ever recorded in North America. That quake caused tsunamis and massive landslides and shifted the elevation and geography of several parts of the state.

When I read about this flourless Earthquake Cake in Anne Byrn's stunning historical cookbook, American Cake, I couldn't think of a better dessert to adapt for this book. The tall outer edges of the cake jut up like snow-dusted mountain peaks, giving way to the shattered ground in the center, dense and rich in chocolate, like moist, moveable earth. The cake, like Alaska, is formidable and stunning to behold, yet imperfect and fragile at the same time. This recipe is a little high maintenance (using your oven timer for precise times will be crucial), but it's also the best flourless chocolate cake I've ever tasted, so it's absolutely worth it.

1 teaspoon unsweetened cocoa powder

10 ounces bittersweet chocolate

½ cup butter

6 eggs, separated

1 cup granulated sugar, divided

3 tablespoons crème de menthe liqueur

FOR SERVING:
Confectioners' sugar

1 Position an oven rack in the center position. Preheat the oven to 375°F. Grease the bottom and sides of an 8" springform pan. Dust the pan with the cocoa.

2 Break the chocolate into pieces and cut the butter into cubes. In a saucepan, combine the chocolate and butter over low heat. Cook, stirring constantly, for 3 minutes, or until the chocolate melts and the mixture becomes smooth. Remove the pan from the heat and set aside.

recipe continues

3 Place the egg yolks in the bowl of a stand mixer fitted with the paddle attachment. Beat on medium-high speed, gradually adding ¾ cup of the granulated sugar. Continue beating for 1 to 2 minutes, or until the yolks are pale yellow and thick. Reduce the mixer speed to the lowest setting and gradually add the chocolate mixture until just combined, scraping the sides and bottom of the bowl as needed. Add the crème de menthe and beat until just combined. Set aside.

4 Add the egg whites to another mixing bowl. Fit the stand mixer with the whisk attachment. Beat on high speed for 2 minutes, or until soft peaks form. Add the remaining ¼ cup granulated sugar and beat for 1 minute, or until stiff peaks form. Using a rubber spatula, gently fold the whites into the chocolate mixture. Pour the batter into the springform pan.

5 Bake the cake for 15 minutes. Reduce the oven temperature to 350°F and bake for 15 minutes. Reduce the oven temperature again to 250°F. Bake for 20 minutes, or until a firm crust forms on top and the cake wiggles slightly to the touch. Turn off the oven, leaving the cake inside. Using a folded kitchen towel, prop open the oven door. Let the cake rest inside the oven with the door propped open for 25 minutes.

6 Move the cake to a wire rack and let cool on the counter for 30 minutes. The cake will collapse as it cools. This is what you want. Gingerly run a butter knife around the edge of the pan before releasing it from the springform sides. Dust the cake with confectioners' sugar. Slice with a sharp knife. Best served warm or at room temperature.

GOLDEN MILK PANNA COTTA WITH PISTACHIOS AND HONEY

Makes 6 servings

I make panna cotta often in the spring and summer months, when I'm looking for a cool dessert recipe that doesn't require turning on the oven. This version has all the flavors of the popular elixir Golden Milk—turmeric, coconut, ginger, cinnamon, cardamom, and a pinch of black pepper. Its vibrant color and exotic aroma draw you in, but you will probably be surprised by this dessert's delicate subtlety. I top it with salted, bright green pistachios and a very light drizzle of local honey.

¼ cup water

2 teaspoons unflavored gelatin powder

1 can (13.5 ounces) unsweetened coconut milk

1 cup half-and-half

½ cup sugar

1 teaspoon ground turmeric

2 cinnamon sticks, snapped in half

1 vanilla bean, slit

Pinch of ground cardamom

Pinch of ground ginger

Pinch of finely ground black pepper

FOR SERVING:

¼ cup roasted salted pistachios, chopped

1 tablespoon honey

1 Lightly oil 6 ramekins.

2 Add the water to a shallow dish. Sprinkle the gelatin powder over the water and allow the gelatin to bloom, about 2 minutes.

3 Meanwhile, in a saucepan, combine the coconut milk, half-and-half, and sugar and heat over medium heat. Add the turmeric, cinnamon sticks, vanilla bean, cardamom, ginger, and pepper. Stir to combine. When the mixture barely starts to simmer, add the gelatin mixture and stir until smooth. Remove the pan from the heat and allow the spices to steep for 5 minutes. Strain the mixture through a fine-mesh sieve. Distribute evenly among the ramekins. Refrigerate for 4 hours.

4 To serve, run a butter knife gingerly around the edges of the panna cotta to loosen. Invert each ramekin onto a separate dessert plate. Sprinkle the tops of the panna cotta with pistachios and drizzle lightly with honey.

KELTY CLAIRE'S PRETZEL BROWNIES

Makes 9

There are 2 brownie camps out there—those who insist upon brownies made with melted chocolate, and those who swear by brownies made with cocoa powder. I'm in the cocoa powder camp all the way. They're undeniably easier, and in my mind, they taste better, too. I like my brownies fudgy and rich, and this one-bowl recipe never lets me down.

Two of my daughter Kelty's favorite snacks are salted pretzels and semisweet chocolate chips. She often turns down a bowl of ice cream for dessert in exchange for a handful of chocolate morsels instead. She's a chocolate-loving girl after my own heart. I adapted my favorite from-scratch brownies with her in mind. I love the crunch and saltiness that the pretzels bring to these brownies. The added chocolate chips melt on top and increase the gooey chocolatey factor. This is the perfect recipe for little kitchen helpers to get involved. Also, try this brownie recipe with other toppings of your choice, like nuts or different morsels. My wife's favorite version has a generous handful of peanut butter chips instead.

½ cup butter, melted

1 cup sugar

2 eggs

1 teaspoon vanilla extract

⅓ cup unsweetened cocoa powder

½ cup all-purpose flour

¼ teaspoon salt

¼ teaspoon baking powder

⅓ cup salted pretzel sticks, roughly chopped

⅓ cup semisweet chocolate chips

1 Preheat the oven to 350°F. Spray a 9" x 9" baking pan with cooking spray.

2 In a mixing bowl, whisk together the butter, sugar, eggs, and vanilla until smooth. Add the cocoa, flour, salt, and baking powder. Stir well to combine.

3 Spread the batter into the baking pan. Sprinkle the top of the brownies with the pretzels and chocolate chips.

4 Bake for 20 to 22 minutes, or until just set but still slightly underdone in the middle, for gooey brownies.

BUTTERSCOTCH BREAD PUDDING

Makes 8 to 10 servings

This isn't your typical bread pudding, the old-fashioned kind made
to use up leftover bread, with raisins, cinnamon, and maybe even nuts. This
is the kind of bread pudding that you crave and make an extra trip to the bakery
to buy a loaf of bread just to make it. This is the kind of bread pudding you take
with you to special events, pulling it out of the oven just before you walk out
the door. This is the kind of bread pudding where people who have sworn off
bread pudding for life will ask you for the recipe. No one will be able to resist the
buttery golden edges, the rich brown sugar custard base, or those gooey
butterscotch chips. Serve it hot with fresh lightly sweetened whipped cream
on top that slowly melts over the pudding and drips down the sides.

1 loaf (about 12–14 ounces)
day-old Italian or French
bread

4 cups whole milk

3 eggs

2 teaspoons vanilla extract

1½ cups firmly packed dark
brown sugar

½ cup butter, melted

¼ teaspoon salt

1 cup butterscotch chips,
divided

FOR SERVING:
Lightly sweetened
whipped cream

1 Preheat the oven to 350°F. Grease a
13" x 9" baking dish.

2 Cut or tear the bread into bite-size
pieces and place them in a large bowl.

2 In a blender, combine the milk, eggs,
vanilla, brown sugar, butter, and salt.
Blend until smooth and well combined.
Pour the custard mixture over the
bread and stir gently to make sure all
the bread is coated. Add ½ cup of the
butterscotch chips and stir gently.
Pour the mixture into the baking dish.
Sprinkle the remaining ½ cup butterscotch chips over top of the bread pudding. Bake for 1 hour, or until golden
brown and puffed up (it should jiggle
when you touch it in the center).

3 Slice into squares and serve warm
with lightly sweetened whipped cream
on top.

RHUBARB COMPOTE
WITH STRAWBERRIES AND ROSÉ

Makes 4 servings

Although often understood to be a spring vegetable, rhubarb grows like a weed here in the summer, thanks to Alaska's relentless sunlight. You can spy rhubarb's massive trademark green leaves and bright red stalks cropping up everywhere around the state. It's so plentiful and hardy in fact that it pretty much grows itself and needs to be given away. I've found anonymous bags full of freshly cut rhubarb from someone's garden sitting at my front door on more than 1 occasion. Many Alaskans keep chopped rhubarb in their freezers that they use throughout the year in all sorts of things, like jams and crumbles and pies.

I love rhubarb for its complex, pucker-worthy acidity and its gorgeous red and pink hues. Simmered down with strawberries, ginger, and a summery rosé wine, it makes a phenomenal warm compote, perfect for topping any buttery shortcake. Don't forget the whipped cream.

2 cups chopped rhubarb

2 cups strawberries, hulled and chopped

½ cup rosé wine

½ cup sugar

2 large slices fresh ginger

In a large saucepan over medium heat, combine the rhubarb, strawberries, wine, sugar, and ginger. Cook until the rhubarb breaks down and the mixture is simmering. Reduce the heat to low and simmer for 10 minutes, or until thickened. Remove the pan from the heat and discard the ginger. Serve the compote warm over shortcake, angel food cake, or pound cake with whipped cream. Or enjoy over vanilla ice cream or stir into plain yogurt.

SOFT AND CHEWY MOLASSES COOKIES

Makes about 2 dozen

Molasses cookies are my son Connor's favorite cookie. He requests them year-round. We aren't talking about gingersnaps, which tend to be thinner and much crunchier than these. I've spent years trying to perfect a soft molasses cookie recipe, attempting to achieve a tender, almost gooey interior and delightfully chewy edges. The thing that always held me up was that most old-fashioned molasses cookies are made with shortening, which gives them that soft texture. I attempted substituting butter instead, but got a crispier cookie with a distinct buttery flavor. Finally, I landed on this version, which uses refined coconut oil in place of shortening, and it's my favorite version yet. The trick is not to overbake them. Take them out when they are still somewhat underdone in the center.

²/₃ cup refined coconut oil, slightly softened

1 cup firmly packed brown sugar

1 egg

½ cup molasses

2⅓ cups all-purpose flour

½ teaspoon salt

1 teaspoon baking soda

1 teaspoon ground ginger

1 teaspoon ground cinnamon

½ teaspoon ground cloves

¼ cup granulated sugar, for rolling the cookies

1 Preheat the oven to 350°F. Line a large baking sheet with parchment paper.

2 In the bowl of a stand mixer fitted with the paddle attachment, cream together the coconut oil and brown sugar. Add the egg and molasses and beat until smooth, scraping the sides and bottom of the bowl as needed. In another mixing bowl, stir together the flour, salt, baking soda, ginger, cinnamon, and cloves. Add the flour mixture to the wet ingredients and beat until completely combined.

3 Using a medium cookie scoop (about 1½ tablespoons), scoop the dough into uniform balls. Roll each ball of dough in granulated sugar before placing it onto the baking sheet. Bake for 7 to 8 minutes, removing them from the oven while they appear still somewhat underdone in the center. As soon as the cookies come out of the oven, press the center of each cookie down with the back of a wooden spoon to achieve a crinkled look. Let the cookies cool on a wire rack; they will become chewier as they cool. Delicious warm or at room temperature.

NUTELLA S'MORES TART

Makes 6 to 8 servings

Campfires and bonfires are a common part of life in rugged and outdoorsy Alaska, and with campfires come s'mores. When I'm making s'mores, one of my pet peeves is when the marshmallows are perfectly golden and oozing inside, but the chocolate squares are cold and hard, as they almost always are. That ruins it for me every single time, although my wife disagrees with me on this and appreciates the firm bite of the chocolate squares.

Several years ago, I developed a solution to my problem: I ditched the milk chocolate squares and swapped them for a generous smear of Nutella. When the hot marshmallow hits the Nutella, melty magic begins to happen. For me, s'mores don't get any more perfect than that. Now I stand by the fire with a jar of Nutella and a butter knife, slathering the chocolate hazelnut spread on everyone's graham crackers as they toast their marshmallows. It's my thing.

This Nutella S'mores Tart recipe is a nod to all the flavors of my favorite campfire s'mores—a buttery graham cracker crust, a rich Nutella filling, and a layer of homemade marshmallow cream browned under the broiler. The result is a crisp, golden marshmallow crust that cracks when sliced, revealing the supple, pure white marshmallow cream underneath. Although my wife and I disagree about what makes the ideal s'more, she declares this tart an absolutely perfect dessert.

recipe continues

FOR THE CRUST:

1¼ cups graham cracker crumbs (see note)

2 tablespoons sugar

4 tablespoons salted butter, melted

FOR THE NUTELLA FILLING:

2 tablespoons cornstarch

2 cups half-and-half, divided

¾ cup Nutella

Pinch of salt

FOR THE MARSHMALLOW CREAM:

½ cup cold water, divided

1 teaspoon unflavored gelatin

¾ cup sugar

¼ cup corn syrup

1 teaspoon vanilla extract

1 *To make the crust:* Preheat the oven to 350°F. Grease a 9" fluted tart pan with a removable bottom.

2 In a mixing bowl, stir together the graham cracker crumbs, sugar, and butter until combined. Press the crust firmly into the bottom and slightly up the sides of the tart pan. Bake for 10 minutes, or until lightly browned and fragrant. Cool on a wire rack.

3 *To make the Nutella filling:* In a small bowl, stir together the cornstarch and ½ cup of the half-and-half. Set aside.

4 In a saucepan over medium heat, combine the Nutella and the remaining 1½ cups half-and-half. Stir in the salt. Heat through, stirring, until the mixture begins to simmer. Stir in the cornstarch mixture. Simmer, stirring constantly, for 3 minutes, or until thickened and smooth. Pour the filling into the graham cracker crust, smoothing it over with an offset spatula. Refrigerate for 2 hours.

5 *To make the marshmallow cream:* Pour ¼ cup of the water into the bowl of a stand mixer fitted with the whisk attachment. Sprinkle the gelatin over top of the water and allow to bloom undisturbed while you continue with the recipe.

6 In a saucepan over high heat, combine the remaining ¼ cup water, the sugar, and corn syrup. Stir until the sugar is dissolved. Bring the mixture to a rolling boil. Cook until it reaches 260°F (known as the hard ball stage) on a candy thermometer. Turn off the heat. Turn the stand mixer on low speed and slowly stream the hot syrup into the bowl with the gelatin mixture. When all of the syrup has been added, gradually increase the mixer speed to high and whip for 5 minutes, or until the mixture turns white and fluffy and doubles in volume. Add the vanilla and whip for 30 seconds to combine. Spread the marshmallow cream on top of the Nutella tart. Return it to the refrigerator for 30 minutes to set.

7 Preheat the broiler to high. Place the tart under the broiler. Watching it carefully and rotating it as needed, toast the top of the tart until golden brown. Remove the tart from the oven and refrigerate for at least 30 minutes.

8 To slice the tart, run a sharp knife under hot water before you begin, and clean off the knife between each cut.

The top of the marshmallow layer will crack when sliced. This is to be expected.

NOTE: I recommend crushing the graham crackers by hand by placing them in a resealable plastic bag and smashing them with a rolling pin. The larger bits of graham cracker evoke the texture of a classic s'more.

MAPLE PECAN CHOCOLATE CHIP COOKIES

Makes about 2 dozen

Everyone loves a reliable, irresistible chocolate chip cookie recipe. If you're not a fan of pecans or nuts in general, feel free to omit them. But don't skip the maple extract either way. It's the secret ingredient that makes these cookies extra special.

³/₄ cup butter, softened

1 cup brown sugar

¹/₂ cup granulated sugar

1 egg

1 egg yolk

1 teaspoon pure vanilla extract

1 teaspoon maple extract

2 cups all-purpose flour

1 teaspoon baking soda

¹/₂ teaspoon salt

1 cup semisweet chocolate chips

¹/₂ cup roasted and salted pecans, roughly chopped

1 Preheat the oven to 325°F. Line 2 large baking sheets with parchment paper.

2 In the bowl of a stand mixer fitted with the paddle attachment, cream together the butter and the sugars. Add the egg and egg yolk and mix to combine. Add the vanilla and maple extracts and mix, scraping the sides and bottom of the bowl as needed.

3 In a bowl, sift together the flour, baking soda, and salt. Add to the sugar mixture and mix until just combined. Add the chocolate chips and pecans and beat until evenly distributed.

4 Using a medium cookie scoop (about 1½ tablespoons), scoop the dough onto the baking sheets. Bake for 12 minutes, or until golden and set on the edges but still a little under-done in the center, being careful not to overbake. The cookies will look puffy when they come out of the oven, but let them rest on the baking sheets for 5 minutes and they will begin to set-tle. Remove the cookies to a wire rack to finish cooling. Best served warm with a glass of milk.

KEY LIME CHEESECAKE WITH PRETZEL CRUST

Makes up to 12 servings

Citrus fruit doesn't grow in Alaska, so I love the time of year when little green bags of adorable Key limes show up in the produce section of the supermarket. It's fun, albeit somewhat tedious, to slice the little buggers and squeeze out all of that precious seasonal juice. Grab the kids or a houseguest to help you with the process. If it's not Key lime season or if you can't find them near you, this recipe also works well with your standard lime.

FOR THE KEY LIME CURD:

3 eggs

¾ cup sugar

¼ cup freshly squeezed Key lime juice

1 teaspoon Key lime zest

1 drop Wilton Leaf Green food coloring gel (optional, see note)

4 tablespoons butter

FOR THE CRUST:

1 cup pretzels, crushed

1 cup graham cracker crumbs

¼ cup sugar

¼ teaspoon salt

8 tablespoons butter, melted

FOR THE CHEESECAKE:

3 blocks (8 ounces each) cream cheese, at room temperature

⅓ cup sour cream

1 can (14 ounces) sweetened condensed milk

3 eggs

2 tablespoons Key lime juice

1 tablespoon Key lime zest

1 *To make the Key lime curd:* In a saucepan, whisk together the eggs and sugar until well combined. Whisk in the Key lime juice, zest, and food coloring gel (if desired).

2 Turn the heat on medium low and stir the mixture briskly and constantly until warmed through. Add the butter a little at a time until it melts into the mixture and becomes smooth. Continue cooking and stirring until the curd begins to thicken and coat the spoon. Pour the curd through a fine-mesh sieve to strain. Transfer to a shallow container. Place a layer of plastic wrap over the curd, touching the top of the curd completely to prevent a layer from forming on top as it cools. Chill in the refrigerator until ready to use. This can be made a day ahead.

recipe continues

3 Preheat the oven to 350°F.

4 *To make the crust:* In a food processor, combine the pretzels and graham crackers. Process until the mixture becomes crumbs. Add the crumbs to a mixing bowl and stir in the sugar, salt, and butter.

5 Grease a 9" springform pan. If your springform pan isn't watertight, wrap the exterior of the pan tightly with foil to prevent water from seeping in while baking.

6 Place a tea kettle of water over high heat and bring to a boil. Have a large, deep baking pan (large enough to hold the springform pan comfortably inside it) ready. I use my 12" cast-iron skillet.

7 Press the crust mixture firmly into the bottom of the springform pan, working it well up the sides. Place the crust in the refrigerator to chill and firm up while you complete the next step.

8 *To make the cheesecake:* Place the cream cheese in the bowl of a stand mixer fitted with the paddle attachment. Beat on medium speed until smooth. Gradually add the sour cream, sweetened condensed milk, eggs, lime juice, and zest. Beat until well combined, scraping the sides of the bowl as needed. Pour the cheesecake filling into the prepared crust, smoothing it evenly with an offset spatula. Place the cheesecake inside the large baking pan. Place the pan in the oven. Carefully pour the hot water into the bottom of the large baking pan to create a water bath about halfway up the outer sides of the springform pan.

9 Bake the cheesecake for 1 hour, or until golden on top and set in the center, wobbling just a bit. Transfer the cheesecake to a wire rack to cool completely. Refrigerate for 4 hours before releasing from the springform pan. Using an offset spatula, spread the Key lime curd on top of the cheesecake. To make clean slices in your cheesecake, wipe the knife off between each pass.

NOTE: I use the tiniest tip of a toothpick of gel, just to give the curd a subtle green tint. This step is completely optional. If you don't use food coloring, the curd will be a creamy yellow, easily mistaken for lemon curd, aside from the flecks of green from the zest.

SUPER PEANUT BUTTER COOKIES

Makes about 2 dozen

I have always been a lover of cookies, but I crave these more than any other type. If you or someone you know has a peanut butter obsession like I do, you are going to want to keep this recipe close by. I took my favorite peanut butter cookie and amped up the peanutty flavor exponentially by using a full cup of extra-crunchy peanut butter and peanut butter chips in the dough.

You might note that I don't put fork marks in my peanut butter cookies. That classic trademark is used as a means to help peanut butter cookies not puff up in the center when baked. I prefer to bake my cookies first, then as soon as they emerge from the oven, still somewhat underdone in the center, I press them down gently using the back of a wooden spoon. This gives them that beautiful crackled look while achieving the same goal as the fork method.

recipe continues

½ cup butter, softened

1 cup extra-crunchy peanut butter

1 cup granulated sugar, divided

½ cup firmly packed brown sugar

1 egg

1 tablespoon whole milk

1 teaspoon vanilla extract

1¼ cups all-purpose flour

¾ teaspoon baking soda

½ teaspoon baking powder

¼ teaspoon salt

¾ cup peanut butter chips

1 Preheat the oven to 350°F. Line a baking sheet with parchment paper.

2 In the bowl of a stand mixer fitted with the paddle attachment, cream together the butter and peanut butter until smooth. Add ¾ cup of the granulated sugar and the brown sugar and cream together until combined. Mix in the egg, followed by the milk and vanilla, scraping the sides and bottom of the bowl as needed.

3 In a mixing bowl, stir together the flour, baking soda, baking powder, and salt. With the mixer on low, gradually add the flour mixture to the peanut butter mixture until thoroughly com-

bined. Add in the peanut butter chips and stir to combine.

4 Using a medium cookie scoop (about 1½ tablespoons), form the dough into balls. Place the remaining ¼ cup granulated sugar in a shallow dish. Roll each ball of dough in the sugar. Place the balls on the baking sheet. Bake for 10 to 12 minutes, being careful not to overbake. The cookies will look slightly underdone in the center, but will set as they cool. Press the top of each cookie down using the back of a wooden spoon to achieve a crinkled look. Allow to cool for 5 minutes before transferring to a wire rack to cool completely.

GRILLED PEACHES WITH SPICED HONEY AND BLACKBERRIES

Makes 4 servings

Stone fruit, so plump and plentiful during my years in California, doesn't grow in Alaska. So when I have the privilege of having some stone fruit in my kitchen, I like to highlight the natural flavors and really allow the fruit to shine.

My favorite fruit pie of all time is blackberry peach. The flavors of that pie inspired this quick dessert recipe of warm grilled peaches drizzled with pie-spiced honey, topped with good, melting vanilla ice cream and sprinkled with juicy blackberries.

4 ripe peaches

3 tablespoons honey

½ teaspoon ground cinnamon

¼ teaspoon ground ginger

Pinch of ground cloves

Pinch of freshly grated nutmeg

Pinch of salt

4 scoops vanilla ice cream

1 pint blackberries

1 Liberally oil a grill pan. Place the pan over medium-high heat. Slice the peaches in half and remove the pits. Place the peaches cut side down on the hot grill pan. Grill for 2 to 4 minutes, turning the peaches 90 degrees halfway through. Remove from the heat and set aside.

2 In a small saucepan over low heat, warm the honey together with the cinnamon, ginger, cloves, nutmeg, and salt. The honey should be smooth and thin enough to drizzle.

3 To assemble, place 2 grilled peach halves cut side up in a bowl. Add a scoop of vanilla ice cream over top of the peaches. Sprinkle with a small handful of blackberries and drizzle with the warm spiced honey. Repeat with the remaining ingredients.

APPLE BROWN BUTTER BLONDIES

—— *Makes 9* ——

While I was in the process of writing this book, my wife would often leave notes for me hidden around the house before leaving for work in the morning. Eventually, I had a whole stack of them tucked behind my baking canisters. They were written in her handwriting on off-white paper, but the words weren't hers. They were excerpts from emails and comments from readers I had received in all my years as a food writer. Not only was she reminding me of words I might have forgotten, but she was also reminding me why I do what I do every day. She was reminding me that there are readers and home cooks and families waiting on the other side of this book. She reminded me that this cookbook would be spread open on kitchen counters, splattered with blondie batter, and working hard alongside you to nourish others and create food memories. She reminded me that it's never just me standing here in the kitchen and that, when it comes to food, we are never alone.

While unassuming and anything but fancy, blondies are one of the quickest, easiest homemade dessert recipes out there. I often whip up a batch of these rich, gooey bars when I'm in a pinch and in need of dessert in a hurry. I make several variations of blondies, keeping the same base recipe and changing up the mix-ins. This time, I added the extra step of browning the butter, and now I wonder why I never did this before. When the browned butter hits the brown sugar and vanilla, the fragrance of butterscotch fills the air. The batter was practically begging me for some tart apples. And finally I added some old-fashioned oats to help soak up the juices from the apple and add a slight chewy texture. I might even dare to suggest serving up a warm blondie with a scoop of vanilla bean ice cream and a sprinkle of sea salt.

½ cup salted butter

1 cup firmly packed brown sugar

1 egg

1 teaspoon vanilla extract

1 cup all-purpose flour

⅓ cup old-fashioned oats

¼ teaspoon salt

1 small tart green apple, cored, peeled, and chopped

1 Preheat the oven to 350°F. Grease a 9" x 9" pan.

2 In a saucepan, cook the butter over medium-high heat until it bubbles up and begins to turn an amber color and becomes fragrant and nutty, being careful not to overcook. Remove the pan from the heat and set aside to cool for 10 minutes.

3 In a mixing bowl, stir together the browned butter and the sugar. Add the egg and vanilla and mix until smooth. Stir in the flour, oats, salt, and apple. Spread the batter into the pan and bake for 20 to 25 minutes, or until set on top and golden on the edges, but still somewhat gooey in the center. Allow the blondies to cool for at least 15 minutes before cutting into bars. Great served warm or at room temperature. Best enjoyed the same day.

ACKNOWLEDGMENTS

TO MY THREE CHILDREN, WHOSE VERY EXISTENCE HAS GIVEN ME ample reason to be in the kitchen every day. It is, and has always been, my privilege to nourish each of you since the moment you were born. To my son Brady, for being my most adventurous and willing eater, for being excited about my food, and for challenging me always. Thank you for loving sushi with me and for putting more creamer in your coffee than even I do. It's nice to know I'm not alone in the world. To my son Connor, for being my pickiest eater, for keeping me humble in the kitchen with your food preferences, and for loving me regardless of whether you'd rather be eating a can of Spaghettios or a bag of popcorn. I love you more. To my daughter, Kelty, my clarity. Thank you for being an enthusiastic helper who climbs on the countertop and stands upon chairs, an opinionated and sassy eater, the bravest soul, my cheerleader, and my encourager.

To my wife, Danae—my hero, my safety, my home. Thank you for being my partner in this and in all things. Your passion and courage inspire me every single day to lean in. Thank you for being the most willing backup photographer, stand-in model, taste-tester, copy editor, dish-washer, grocery-picker-upper, and sanity-giver. Thank you for all the notes of encouragement you secretly left for me throughout this long process that reminded me day in and day out why I do what I do. Thank you for being the one who sees me and for reminding me to sit at my own table every single day. I would not be who I am today without you and your fierce love.

To Jacob James, there are no words adequate enough to thank you; I'd have to write another book. But, as has always been true with us, I don't need to say it. You already know. Thank you for believing that I am one of those badass women worth fighting for. To Jeffrey Robinson, an incredible attorney and human being. Both of you helped make this possible.

To Kim Sunée, for your unrivaled generosity of spirit, your impeccable taste, your rich hospitality, and your constant friendship. Your story and the ways in which you fearlessly share it have given me the courage to put myself out there, too. Thank you for helping me along the way, particularly when I needed to be reminded that I have what it takes, which was often. Thank you for writing the exquisite foreword to this book. Thank you also for sharing your table with me, and for introducing me to fine food and drinks, and to even finer people. I still cannot believe our paths crossed in Alaska, of all places, but I am forever grateful that they did.

To Joy Tutela, my phenomenal agent, at the David Black Agency in New York. Thank you for lighting a fire under my ass precisely when I needed it most. Thank you for all of the ways you believed in this book and fought for it. We may be 4,000 miles apart, but I know you're always there at the other end of my emails. I wouldn't be here without your expertise and your wisdom. Thank you for being my advocate.

Enormous thanks to the Alaska Seafood Marketing Institute and to Kate Consenstein at Rising Tide Communications for supplying me with the world-class seafood in this book. It is a privilege to get to work with such high-quality, fresh, local ingredients. Your seafood is not only sensational in flavor and insanely fresh, but it's also beautifully photogenic. I cannot thank you enough for partnering with me on this project and helping me bring

Alaska seafood to life in these pages.

A big shout-out to Erickson Woodworks for their excellent work creating the boards for most of the photo backdrops in this book.

Massive props to my logo designer, Diane Tusi. Thank you for understanding my aesthetic and contributing your talent to *Alaska from Scratch*.

To Jeff and Liz Wilson, for recipe-testing cocktails for me for this book and for sharing your kitchen and your lives with me. I'm so thankful we're family. To Kristen and Marie LoPrell: thank you for being the ones who text and call with questions mid-recipe and who include me in your meal planning and in your lives. Thank you for being a part of the journey of this book from the outset. To Chris True, for teaching me a thing or two about steak and for your stellar marinade recipe.

To Kari Amador Ludovina, my longtime best friend, for being there through it all. Also, thank you for introducing me to pupusas, curtido, and plantanos. My life has never been the same. To Bill and Erin McCoy, who actively read and cooked along from the beginning of my blog, *Alaska from Scratch,* sending me feedback along the way. Thank you all for more than 20 years of eating and sharing life together.

To Luke Thibodeau, Chef Kenneth Hynes, and the whole crew, front of the house and back, at The Flats Bistro in Kenai, Alaska. Thank you for believing in me, working alongside me, and helping transform a timid self-taught home cook into a confident line cook and brunch chef. I'd gladly be in the weeds with you any day.

To Karen DeSollar, who, when I worked in her office at the age of 18, told me assuredly that I would be a writer and that one day she would be reading my book. To Tim Lundin, who many years ago was the first to suggest I seriously consider a career in food.

To the board of directors of Peninsula Community Health Services of Alaska, thank you for giving me a seat at your table and offering me a place to have a voice and give back to our community while I was in the process of writing this book.

Thank you to the Wells Fargo branch in Soldotna, Alaska, for helping make this book a reality.

A giant nod to the Kenai River Queens hockey team. Thank you for rooting for me and this book the way I root for you on the ice.

Big thanks to to K2 Aviation, Denali ATV Adventures, and Denali Zipline Tours in Talkeetna, Alaska, Pilot Deb Moseley and Steller Air, True North Kayak Adventures in Homer, Alaska, Phillips Glacier Cruises in Whittier, Alaska, Kenai Fjords National Park in Seward, Alaska, Kasilof Historical Museum, the Kenai National Wildlife Refuge, Kachemak Bay State Park, Denali National Park and Preserve, Katmai National Park and Preserve, and Airbnb. Thank you also to all of the Alaska towns featured in this book: Hope, Cooper Landing, Kenai, Soldotna, Homer, Kasilof, Nikiski, Ninilchik, Whittier, Seward, Sterling, Anchor Point, and Talkeetna.

To the entire Rodale team. What a remarkable group of women you are. To Dervla Kelly, my brilliant editor - I knew we clicked during our first conversation. You asked such thoughtful questions and our visions for this book really resonated with each other. I knew right away that I was in very capable hands with you and with Rodale. It's been a complete privilege to work with you and such fun, too. Thank you for believing in me and my work. To Rae Ann Spitzenberger, my amazing designer. You rock. You're great at what you do. Thank you for getting my vibe and making this book more beautiful than I ever imagined. To Anna Cooperberg, editorial assistant, and Aly Mostel and Susan Turner in PR. Thank you for being delightful human beings to work with. Thank you also to Angie Giammarino in marketing and Marilyn Hauptly in managing editorial. Each one of you has helped make my dreams come true. I can't thank you enough. It is an absolute honor to be a Rodale author.

To all of the *Alaska from Scratch* readers, followers, and fans. Thank you for sitting with me.

INDEX

Boldfaced page references indicate photographs.